Welcome to HeartShaper®

Shaping Hearts with God's Word

Thank you for choosing HeartShaper Children's Curriculum. Beginning this quarter, you'll find MORE and NEW resources designed to help you:

REACH kids with special needs

a quarterly newsletter that teachers can use for adapting lessons and including children who have special needs.

- General tips and encouragement for teachers
- Age-specific ways to adapt activities included in HeartShaper lessons
- Ideas for helping families of children with special needs

LEAD kids to Christ

a pocket guide designed to help teachers and volunteers lead a child to a salvation decision.

- Quick reference for teachers including tips for where to start and what to ask kids
- Scripture references to help a child learn what it means to have a personal relationship with Jesus
- Ideas to guide children through God's Word and provide ongoing encouragement

CONNECT with HeartShaper community

a resourceful website including discussion forums with topics relevant to children's ministry leaders, teachers, and volunteers.

Ask questions, share ideas, and get connected!

TRAIN yourself and your team

online resources including free downloads, recruiting and training videos, PowerPoint presentations, and more!

Feel confident teaching HeartShaper lessons right from the start!

Learn more at heartshaper.com

How to Use **HeartShaper**®

- Read the introductory pages and the unit pages.
- Use the correlated HeartShaper materials.
- Pray for God's help to guide children to a personal relationship with Jesus Christ.

Quick Step activities are easy to prepare.

Use all the activities in **Step 2**.

Optional activities are included in **Steps 1, 3, and 4.**

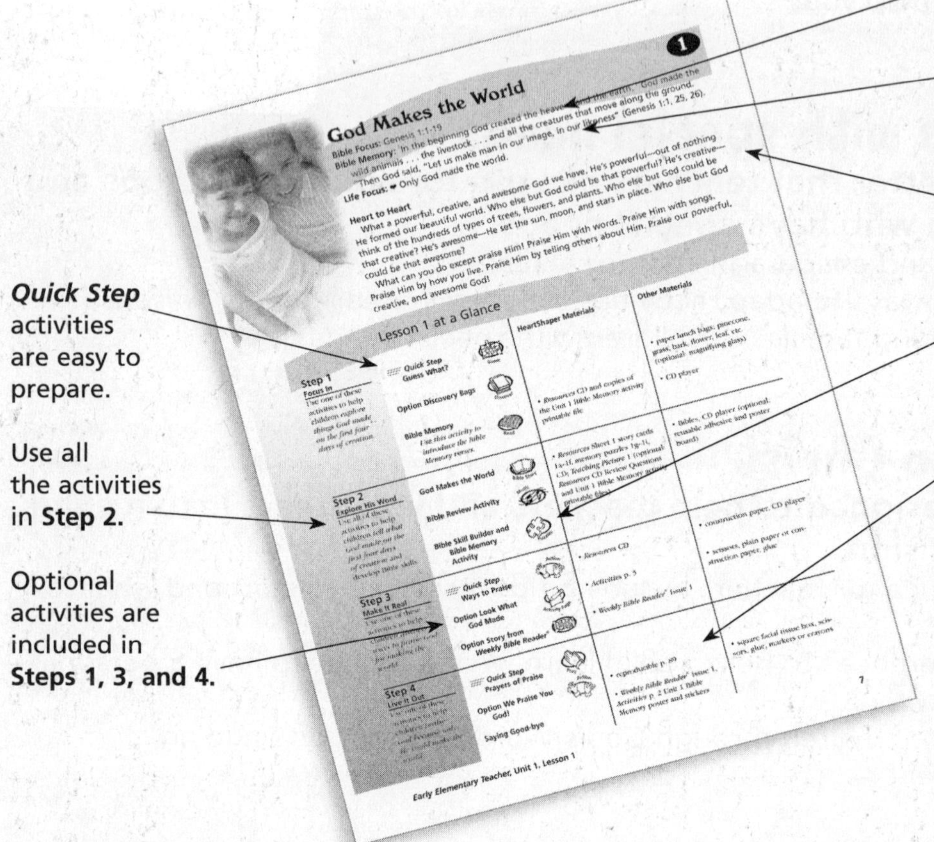

Bible Memory for children to learn.

Life Focus is the main thought children will learn and remember.

Heart to Heart provides inspirational thoughts for teachers.

Activity icons identify at a glance the types of activities offered.

Materials included in HeartShaper curriculum.

Special Note
If you are part of a rotating team of teachers, meet together to pray and plan. Work together on developing a basic schedule for class sessions, establishing class rules and consequences, planning service projects and parties, and decorating the room.

Step 1 Focus In: Children explore the lesson theme and are introduced to the Bible Memory.

Step 2 Explore His Word: Children explore what the Bible says, learn Bible skills, and learn Bible Memory verses.

Step 3 Make It Real: Children discover how the lessons learned from the Bible relate to their lives.

Step 4 Live It Out: Children either *do* what has been learned or plan *how* to do it.

You can adapt this curriculum!

- Use this curriculum with a large group/small group format. You could do Steps 1, 3, and 4 in small groups and Step 2 in a large group.
- Use this curriculum with a team approach. Have different team members plan and lead activities in each of the steps.
- For additional learning activities, use more than one activity option per step.
- Use unused options for a weekday program.

Early Elementary Teacher

Have a Plan

Online Helps
- A modifiable newsletter is available online to help you connect with families of children in your class.
- Look for seasonal and holiday ideas to help children remember God and celebrate Jesus all year long.
- Apply the online training tips to your teaching and grow in your effectiveness to reach today's kids with God's Word.

Go to **heartshaper.com**.

HeartShaper E-news
Sign up to receive a weekly newsletter with expert tips and free downloads you can use in the classroom. Go to heartshaper.com.

Shaping hearts with God's Word

● Plan ahead.
Prepare your room with basic supplies, age-appropriate furniture, and interesting things to look at. Do you need an offering container, *New International Version* classroom Bibles, additional activity books, a CD player, or a first-aid kit? Plan to be in class before the first child arrives.

● Plan for classroom management.
Before class, give enough time to preparation. Understand the characteristics of early elementary children and teach accordingly. Pray for yourself and the children you teach. During class, show the children that you care about them. Know their names and use them. Never raise your voice. Post rules and make sure children understand why certain behaviors are unacceptable. Always expect good behavior.

● Plan to be safe.
Know your church's security guidelines and follow them. You should have guidelines about dismissing children, teacher-to-child ratios, and restroom breaks. Know the location of first-aid supplies. Before you serve snacks, be aware of any allergies children may have. Make sure you have plans for what to do when a fire alarm sounds or in the case of severe weather. Know where each child's parents or guardians are during the time children are in class.

● Plan to include all children.
Some of the children in your class will be from single-parent homes, blended families, and/or foster homes. Some children may have more than one mother or father figure. Be sensitive to each child's situation. Some children may have disabilities. Learn about the child's disability. Plan to include the child in all activities and show him the unconditional love of Jesus.

● Plan to lead children to Jesus.
Remember that all your plans should lead in only one direction—to Jesus. Plan and pray that all you do will help lay the foundation for a child to have a lifelong relationship with Jesus Christ.

Basic Supplies Needed
Books and equipment
- *NIV* Bibles, white board and dry-erase markers, erasers, bulletin board and pushpins, CD player, stapler, rulers, scissors, hole punch, beanbags

Consumable materials
- markers, crayons, colored pencils, pencils, dry-erase markers, plain paper, card stock, construction paper, roll paper, poster board, index cards, clear tape, glue, reusable adhesive, yarn, staples, craft sticks, paper towels, old magazines, paper fasteners

Leading Kids to Jesus
One of the greatest joys of teaching is the opportunity to participate with kids as they begin thinking about salvation decisions. A "Leading Young Hearts to the Lord" Pocket Guide is included on the *Resources* CD. Print and keep a copy handy so that you will be prepared whenever the opportunity arises to discuss this important matter.

Bible Skills

As you teach the lessons in this book, you will be helping the kids in your class develop the ability to study God's Word and find for themselves God's answers for the everyday situations they face. Bible skills activities are intentionally integrated into each lesson.

EARLY ELEMENTARY children will . . .

September   Know the Bible has an Old Testament and a New Testament. Understand the difference between the Old Testament and New Testament.

October   Understand what a Scripture reference means.

November   Name Old Testament main characters.

December   Use the table of contents to find a testament.

January   Use the table of contents to find a book.

February   Name New Testament main characters.

March   Review the difference between the Old Testament and New Testament.

April   Review what a Scripture reference means.

May   Name the first four books in the New Testament.

June   Review using a table of contents to find a book.

July   Name the first five books of the Old Testament.

August   Review all Bible skills.

Ongoing Skills   Find verses in the Bible.
Begin to read Bible verses.
Memorize selected Bible verses.

Shaping hearts with God's Word

God Helps David

Lesson	Bible Focus	Life Focus
Lesson 1 David Does His Job	David, the shepherd boy. 1 Samuel 16, 17	⊠ God helps us do our jobs.
Lesson 2 David Is Brave	David and Goliath. 1 Samuel 17	⊠ God helps us be brave.
Lesson 3 David and Jonathan Are Friends	The friendship between David and Jonathan. 1 Samuel 18–20	⊠ God helps us be friends.
Lesson 4 David Does the Right Thing	David spares King Saul's life. 1 Samuel 26	⊠ God helps us do right things.

Bible Memory

Psalms 124:8; 146:5

Our help is in the name of the LORD, the Maker of heaven and earth.

Blessed are those whose help is the God of Jacob, whose hope is in the LORD their God.

Print the KJV *or* NIV *Additional Bible Memory file from the* Resources *CD for more Bible Memory verses kids will enjoy learning.*

Bible Skills for Unit 1

Children will

- know the Bible has an Old Testament and a New Testament.
- understand the basic difference between the Old Testament and New Testament.

Ongoing Bible Skills

Children will

- find verses in the Bible.
- begin to read Bible verses.
- memorize selected Bible verses.

Life Skills for Unit 1

Children will

- ask God for His help.
- desire to do right things.
- thank God for His help.

HeartShaper Materials for Unit 1

Early Elementary Activities, **Lessons 1–4 and the Unit 1 Bible Memory Poster and Stickers**

Early Elementary Teaching Pictures, **Lessons 1–4**

Early Elementary Resources

CD

"Happy Are Those," Tracks 1, 2

"Show My Love," Tracks 5, 6

"A Scary Day," story for Lesson 2, Track 8

Bible Story for Lesson 4, Track 9

Bible Memory: *KJV* or *NIV* Additional Bible Memory for Unit 1, *New International Version* Bible Memory for Unit 1, *King James Version* Bible Memory for Unit 1

Bible Skills Worksheets, Unit 1

Buzzy Bee Letters, Lessons 1–4

Worship Time Ideas, Unit 1

Review Questions, Unit 1

Letter to Families, Unit 1

Posters and Activities: God Helps David book cover, Books of the Old Testament posters, Books of the New Testament posters

Teacher Helps: Attendance Chart, Discipline and Classroom Management, Early Elementary Children, Leading Young Hearts Guide, Safety and Security Issues, Starting the New Year, Transition Tips

Visuals

Sheet 1 Bible Memory poster, story figures 3a–3e, 4a, 4b; Sheet 2 David name card, animal photos 1a–1c, story figures 2a–2f; Sheet 3 photo cards

Weekly Bible Reader®, **Issues 1–4**

Faith & Family **online resource**

A weekly devotional guide for parents and kids to use together.

Go to heartshaper.com.

Use these activities for early arrivers, for children who finish activities quickly, and when you are waiting for parents to arrive.

"Our Help" Bulletin Board

Enlarge the globe from the narrow column to fill a bulletin board. Create this title in outline letters: "Our help is in the name of the Lord, the Maker of heaven and earth" (Psalm 124:8). Let the children color the globe and the letters. Let the kids mount the globe on a bulletin board and put the title around the globe.

Getting to Know You

As a new Sunday school year begins, use one of these activities to help you get to know the children and to help the children get to know each other.

People Outlines

Give each child a large paper outline of a person. Tell the children to draw pictures or find pictures in magazines that show things they like to do, food they like to eat, and other favorite things. Let kids talk about their favorite things and display the people outlines in your room.

Favorites

Prepare a large circle for each child. Divide the circle into seven sections and write one of these titles in each section: My name; Favorite toy; Favorite food; Favorite book; Favorite color; Favorite movie; Favorite book. Give the children the circles and guide them to draw or write their favorite things. Let the children show their completed circles. Then display them in your room.

Fun, Add-on Drawings

Let three or four kids work together on these drawings. Kids could draw David, Goliath, Jonathan, and/or King Saul. Have the first child draw a circle on a sheet of paper. This is the head. That child passes the paper to the next child. The next child draws two eyes on the head. The next child draws a mouth. The children continue adding to the picture until it is completed.

A Sweet Welcome

For a fun way to welcome children to your class, write or type the following and copy onto colorful paper: "It is **M**agnificent **and M**arvelous fun having you in our class!" Fill a resealable plastic bag with M&M's® chocolate candies for each child. Then attach the bags to the paper. Kids will love the sweet welcome. You can also let the children prepare these to have available as there are guests in your class.

Bible Skills

Make copies of the Bible Skills Worksheets for Unit 1 from the *Resources* CD. For Unit 1, children will know the Bible has an Old Testament and a New Testament and understand the basic difference between the Old Testament and New Testament.

Teaching Tip

For more ideas on making this new quarter special, see the Teacher Helps "Starting the New Year" printable file on the *Resources* CD. For a fun fall craft idea, go to www.heartshaper.com and check out the teacher resources under Downloads.

David Does His Job

Bible Focus: 1 Samuel 16:11, 18; 17:34-37
Bible Memory: Our help is in the name of the LORD, the Maker of heaven and earth (Psalm 124:8). Blessed are those whose help is the God of Jacob, whose hope is in the LORD their God (Psalm 146:5).
Life Focus: ⊠ God helps us do our jobs.

Heart to Heart

David was a shepherd, which meant he took care of sheep. It doesn't sound like a very glamorous job or one that came with a large salary or many perks, does it? But God was with David and helped David be the best shepherd he could be.

Just like David, God has given you a shepherding job to do which may not be very glamorous and does not come with many perks. But the little lambs that you teach and guide are very important to God. God will be with you. Allow Him to help you do your job and become the best shepherd you can be.

Lesson 1 at a Glance

Step 1		HeartShaper Materials	Other Materials
Focus In Use one of these activities to help children *explore jobs people do.*	*Quick Step* **Jobs People Do** 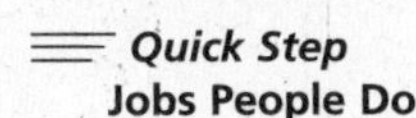	• *Activities* p. 3	• none
	Option Jobs in the Bag 	• none	• pencil, car keys, hammer, bandage or stethoscope, toy, toy animal, large bag
	Bible Memory *Use this activity to introduce the Bible Memory verses.* 	• none	• Bible

Step 2			
Explore His Word Use all of these activities to help children *tell how God helped David do his job* and develop Bible skills.	**David Does His Job** 	• *Resources* Sheet 2 David name card and animal photos 1a–1c, CD God Helps David book cover and Review Questions Unit 1 printable files, Sheet 1 Bible Memory poster; *Teaching Picture* 1; *Activities* p. 4	• white board, dry-erase marker, Bibles, construction paper, reusable adhesive, hole punch, yarn or rings, pencils
	Bible Review Activity 		
	Bible Skill Builder and Bible Memory Activity 		

Step 3			
Make It Real Use one of these activities to help children *list ways God helps people do their jobs.*	*Quick Step* **With God's Help** 	• *Activities* p. 3	• white board, dry-erase marker
	Option How Does God Help? 	• none	• pencil, car keys, hammer, bandage or stethoscope, toy, toy animal, large bag, white board, dry-erase marker
	Option Story from *Weekly Bible Reader®* 	• *Weekly Bible Reader®* Issue 1	• none

Step 4			
Live It Out Use one of these activities to help children *ask for God's help to do their jobs.*	*Quick Step* **Prayers for God's Help** 	• none	• none
	Option Job Wheels 	• reproducible p. 89, *Resources* CD	• markers, CD player, scissors, hole punch, yarn or ribbon
	Saying Good-bye 	• *Weekly Bible Reader®* Issue 1 and the *Activities* p. 2 Unit 1 Bible Memory poster and stickers	• none

Focus In (15 minutes)

Step 1 • Use one of these activities to help children **explore jobs people do.**
Use the Bible Memory activity to introduce the memory verses.

Welcome
- Welcome each child by name.
- Do check-in procedures you follow (name and security tags, offering, attendance chart, etc.).
- Early arrivers will enjoy doing one or more of the activities described on page 6.

≡ *Quick Step* Jobs People Do

Let's think about the many different jobs people do. Distribute the activity pages. Read the directions aloud. Have the children tell what jobs the people in the photos do. (doctor, astronaut, raising a family, student with homework, veterinarian, barber, teacher, firefighter)
- **What are some things a doctor does at his job?**
- **What are some things a veterinarian does at her job?** Ask the same questions for all the jobs pictured.
- **What are some other jobs people do?** (builder, work in an office, housework, minister, yard work, and so forth)
- **What other jobs do people in your family do?**
- **What jobs do you do?**

There are lots of jobs people can do. And there is someone who helps us do our jobs. We're going to learn that ⊠ **God helps us do our jobs.**

Materials
Activities p. 3

Activity Page

Added Fun!
Let kids take turns acting out jobs people do. The rest of the class can guess what the jobs are.

Option Jobs in the Bag

Let's think about the many different jobs people do. Before class, put the items into a large bag. Show children the bag and have a child reach into the bag and pull out one item. Ask that child to tell what kind of job a person might do using that item. (pencil—office worker or teacher; keys—bus driver; hammer—builder; bandage—nurse or doctor; toy—preschool teacher or mom and dad; toy animal—veterinarian or zookeeper)
- **What are some other jobs people do?** (builder, work in an office, housework, minister, raising a family, yard work, and so forth)
- **What other jobs do people in your family do?**
- **What jobs do you do?**

There are lots of jobs people can do. And there is someone who helps us do our jobs. We're going to learn that ⊠ **God helps us do our jobs.**

Materials
pencil, car keys, hammer, bandage or stethoscope, toy, toy animal, large bag

Discover

Bible Memory Psalms 124:8; 146:5

Let's think about things we may need help with. Raise your hand if you sometimes need help cleaning your room. Ask a few kids with their hands raised to tell who helps them clean their rooms. **Raise your hand if you sometimes need help with schoolwork.** Ask a few kids to tell who helps them with schoolwork. **Raise your hand if you sometimes need help doing jobs at home, school, or church.** Ask a few kids to tell who helps them with their jobs. Read aloud Psalms 124:8 and 146:5. **According to these verses of Scripture, who helps us?** (the Lord) **We're going to learn that** ⊠ **God helps us do our jobs.**

Materials
Bible

Transition to Explore His Word
See the *Resources* CD Transition Tips printable file. As children gather, make sure you have all the materials you need.

Life Focus
☒ God helps us do our jobs.

Explore His Word (20 minutes)

Step 2 • Use all of these activities to help children **tell how God helped David do his job** and develop Bible skills.

Bible Background for the Teacher

As was common for the youngest son in a family, David's job was watching the sheep that belonged to his family. David's experiences as a shepherd prepared him for other jobs God gave him later in his life. The duties of a shepherd included leading his flock to grass and water and, when necessary, rescuing sheep from predators, such as lions and bears. As Israel's king, David would later care for God's people and fight their enemies. Spending so much time with his sheep gave David detailed knowledge of Israel's countryside, which would later be of value in his military campaigns. David's talent of harp playing allowed him to regularly play for King Saul and introduced David to palace life and government.

A shepherd's chief weapons were his wooden club and a sling. A sling consisted of a piece of leather with a thin strap attached on each end. Placing a stone on the leather, the shepherd would hold both straps and whirl the sling round and round before releasing one of the straps, hurling the stone at the intended target. A shepherd's sling was also used to toss stones near wandering sheep to startle them back into the flock.

Worship Time

If you want to offer a time of worship, see the *Resources* CD Worship Time Ideas printable file for suggestions.

Materials

white board; dry-erase marker; Bibles; *Resources* Sheet 2 David name card and animal photos 1a–1c; 4 sheets of construction paper; reusable adhesive; *Teaching Picture* 1; hole punch; yarn or rings (optional: *Resources* CD printable files cover for book about David)

Before Class

Have four sheets of construction paper ready to begin making the book about David's life. You can print a colorful cover for the book from the *Resources* CD printable files.

David Does His Job   (1 Samuel 16:11, 18; 17:34-37)

Our Bible story comes from the book of 1 Samuel. The Bible is divided into two main sections, the Old Testament and the New Testament. Write "1 Samuel 16:11" on the board. **First Samuel is in the Old Testament.** Help children find 1 Samuel 16:11 in their Bibles. Ask for a volunteer to read the verse.

Choose a child to hold up the "David" name card when David's name is mentioned. Then that child gives the name card to another child. That child holds up the name card the next time David's name is mentioned. Continue this throughout the story. At the appropriate times, attach the sheep, lion, and bear photos to separate sheets of construction paper with reusable adhesive.

We are going to make a book about the life of David as we learn about him in our Bible stories. Watch as we begin to make our book and listen for how God helped David do his job.

David had been chosen by God to be the next king of Israel after Saul. And Samuel had anointed **David** as the new king even though he was still a boy. But **David** didn't become the king of Israel right away.

The job **David** did helped prepare him to one day be the king of Israel. As a boy, he had one main job. He was a shepherd. *(Show* Teaching Picture *1.)* That meant that **David** took care of the sheep that belonged to his father Jesse. *(Attach the sheep photo to a sheet of construction paper. Hold it up for all to see.)* Each morning, **David** would get up very early and take the sheep out into the hills to find good green grass for them to eat. He also had to keep the sheep safe. When the sheep fell into holes, he would have to pull them out. **David** also had to find water for the sheep to drink and shade for them to rest in.

(Attach the lion photo to a sheet of construction paper. Hold it up for all to see.) One time, a lion came near **David's** flock of sheep and carried off one of the sheep. **David** went after the lion. He struck it, and the sheep was able to get away from the lion. Then **David** grabbed the lion by its hair, struck the lion, and killed it.

(Attach the bear photo to a sheet of construction paper. Hold it up for all to see.) Another time, a bear came near **David's** flock of sheep and carried off

one of the sheep. **David** went after the bear. Just as with the lion, he struck the bear, and the sheep got away. The **David** grabbed it by its hair, struck the bear, and killed it.

David knew that the Lord God had helped him kill both the lion *(hold up the page with the lion photo)* and the bear *(hold up the page with the bear photo)*. God had given **David** strength and courage to do his job as a shepherd *(hold up the page with the sheep photo)*.

Bible Review Activity

What was David's job when he was a boy? (shepherd) **How did God help David do his job?** (God helped David be brave. God helped David care for his sheep by helping David kill a lion and a bear.) **Let's see what else you remember from the Bible story.** Distribute the activity pages and pencils. Read the directions aloud and do the page together.

Then play a fun review game. Have the kids sit on the floor in a circle. Choose one child to be the shepherd. The shepherd walks around the outside of the circle gently touching each child on the head. The shepherd says "sheep" as he touches each child's head, except for one child the shepherd touches and says "lion." The child called lion stands up and chases the shepherd around the outside of the circle back to the lion's place. If the lion tags the shepherd before the shepherd sits down, ask the shepherd a question about the Bible story. If the lion does not tag the shepherd, ask the lion a question using the Review Questions. The lion then takes a turn being the shepherd.

God helped David do his job as a shepherd. We're learning that ⊠ God helps us do our jobs too!

Bible Skill Builder and Bible Memory Activity

Hold up a Bible. **The Bible is divided into two main sections, the Old Testament and the New Testament. The Old Testament tells about God making the world. The New Testament tells about Jesus being born.** Write "Psalm 124:8" and "Psalm 146:5" on the board. **The book of Psalms is in the Old Testament.** Have children look in the table of contents in the front of their Bibles. Help them find the Old Testament section and tell them to run their fingers down the list until they see the book of Psalms. Help children find the two memory verses and ask for volunteers to read the verses.

Display the Bible Memory poster. Read the words while pointing to them. Pause when you come to an empty space and ask who knows what word is missing. When a child says the right word, let him press out that word or picture from the bottom of the poster and attach it to the poster with reusable adhesive. When all the spaces have been filled, lead the kids in saying together the memory verses.

David knew that the Lord God helped him do his job as a shepherd. We know that ⊠ God helps us do our jobs too!

Life Focus

⊠ God helps us do our jobs.

Make It Real (15 minutes)

Step 3 • Use one of these activities to help children **list ways God helps people do their jobs.**

Materials

Activities p. 3, white board, dry-erase marker

Expert Tip

"Our challenge in children's ministry today is to introduce the children to a real God who has real things to say that will really help children in their real world."

—*Steve Alley*

Materials

pencil, car keys, hammer, bandage or stethoscope, toy, toy animal, large bag, white board, dry-erase marker

Materials

Weekly Bible Reader® Issue 1

≡ *Quick Step* With God's Help

We've learned that God helped David do his job as a shepherd. Let's think about how ⊠ God helps us do our jobs. Distribute the activity pages. Put the children in pairs or small groups. Assign one or two of the pictured jobs to each group. The children are to discuss how God might help people doing those jobs. Be prepared to give the children some ideas. After a few minutes, ask each group to share their ideas while you write their ideas on the board.

• **How might God help a person who has the job of being a doctor?** (help him do his best, help him learn more things to do his job better)

• **How might God help a person who has the job of being a student?** (help him do his best, help him remember what he's studying, help him be honest)

• **How might God help a person who has the job of being a firefighter?** (help by keeping him safe, help him be brave)

• **How does God help you do your jobs?**

Ask each group a similar question. **There are lots of jobs people do and most jobs are rather hard. I'm glad that ⊠ God helps us do our jobs.**

Option How Does God Help?

We've learned that God helped David do his job as a shepherd. Let's think about how ⊠ God helps us do our jobs. Before class, if you did not do the "Jobs in the Bag" activity in Step 1, gather the items and put them in a bag. Ask a child to reach into the bag and pull out one of the items. If the child pulls out a pencil, ask:

• **How could God help a child be a better student?** (help him to do his best, help him remember what he's studying, help him be honest)

Write the responses on the board. Continue letting children pull out items from the bag and asking them questions such as:

• **How could God help a builder do his job?** (help him by keeping him safe, help him learn more to do his job better, help him be honest)

There are lots of jobs people do and most jobs are rather hard. I'm glad that ⊠ God helps us do our jobs.

Option Story from *Weekly Bible Reader®*

We've learned that God helped David do his job as a shepherd. Let's think about how ⊠ God helps us do our jobs. Read "Alison Works Hard."

• **What are some ways God helps us do our jobs?** (keeps us safe, helps us be brave, helps us do the best we can do, helps us tell the truth, helps us work hard, helps us be honest)

There are lots of jobs people do and most jobs are rather hard. I'm glad that ⊠ God helps us do our jobs.

Step 4 • Use one of these activities to help children **ask for God's help to do their jobs.**

Quick Step   Prayers for God's Help

We've learned that ⌧ God helps us do our jobs. We just have to ask for His help. Have the children gather in a circle. Ask each child to name one job he does. Then lead the children in a time of directed prayer. Tell children that you will be giving them ideas of what to silently pray about. Be sure to pray about the jobs the children have named.

Dear God, thank You for the jobs we have. If you have the job of taking out the trash, ask for God's help. (pause for a short time) **If you have the job of washing dishes, ask for God's help.** (pause for a short time) **If you have the job of doing schoolwork, ask for God's help.** (pause for a short time) **If you have the job of cleaning your room, ask for God's help.** (pause for a short time) **Thank You, God, for helping us with all our jobs. In Jesus' name, amen.**

Option   Job Wheels

We've learned that ⌧ God helps us do our jobs. We just have to ask for His help. We are going to make job wheels that will help us remember to ask for God's help doing our jobs. Before class, make copies of the reproducible page. Distribute the pages and markers. Read the directions aloud and encourage kids to draw or write about jobs they do. As they work, you can play "Happy Are Those." As children finish their jobs wheels, help them cut out the wheels, punch holes, and string with yarn.

When all the children are finished, have them bring their job wheels to a closing prayer circle. Invite the children to show what they have drawn or talk about one or two jobs they have. **In the middle of your job wheels is a prayer: "God, help me do my jobs. Thanks!" We're going to pray that prayer and ask for God's help in doing our jobs.** Ask kids to silently pray and ask for God's help doing their jobs. After a short time of silent prayer, close with prayer. **Dear God, thank You for our jobs. Help us do our jobs. In Jesus' name, amen.**

Saying Good-bye

• Distribute Issue 1 of *Weekly Bible Reader®* and the *Activities* page 2 Unit 1 Bible Memory poster and stickers. Stickers are in the middle of *Early Elementary Activities*. Encourage kids to complete their posters at home.

• Make sure children have projects and activity sheets they have done.

• If you have time before parents arrive, use some of the activities on page 6.

• Be sure parents know about the *Faith & Family* page available online to download and use at home. You may want to print and have a copy on display for parents to see. Go to heartshaper.com.

Materials
none

Added Fun!
Play "Show My Love" from the *Resources* CD Tracks 5 and 6. Invite kids to join in. Remind kids that it's good to both say and show God that we love Him.

Materials
reproducible p. 89, markers, *Resources* CD Tracks 1 and 2, CD player, scissors, hole punch, yarn or ribbon

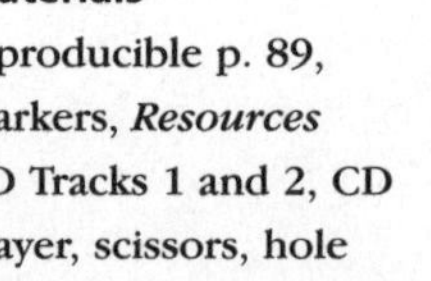

Teaching Tip
Copying the wheel onto card stock will make it sturdier for hanging.

Evaluate
• How well did the children understand the need to ask for God's help doing their jobs?

• How did you help all children feel welcome?

David Is Brave

2

Bible Focus: 1 Samuel 17:1-52
Bible Memory: Our help is in the name of the LORD, the Maker of heaven and earth (Psalm 124:8). Blessed are those whose help is the God of Jacob, whose hope is in the LORD their God (Psalm 146:5).
Life Focus: ⊠ God helps us be brave.

Heart to Heart

David was only a boy, but he was brave because he knew God was with him. Are you brave and remember that God is with you when you are faced with financial problems? Are you brave and remember that God is with you when you are faced with a medical crisis? Are you brave and remember that God is with you when you are faced with family problems?

You don't have to have a certain profession or be a certain age to be brave. You only need to know that God is with you and that He will be your help.

Lesson 2 at a Glance

Step 1 **Focus In** Use one of these activities to help children *define what it means to be brave.*	*Quick Step* **Bravery Jump Up**	HeartShaper Materials • none	Other Materials • none
	Option Being Brave	• *Resources* Sheet 3 Lesson 2 photo cards	• beanbag or soft ball, CD player
	Bible Memory *Use this activity to introduce the Bible Memory verses.*	• none	• Bible
Step 2 **Explore His Word** Use all of these activities to help children *describe a time God helped David be brave* and develop Bible skills.	**David Is Brave**	• *Resources* Sheet 2 David name card and figures 2a–2f, CD; book about David begun in Lesson 1; *Teaching Picture* 2; *Activities* p. 5	• white board, dry-erase marker, Bibles, construction paper, reusable adhesive, markers, scissors, CD player
	Bible Review Activity		
	Bible Skill Builder and Bible Memory Activity		
Step 3 **Make It Real** Use one of these activities to help children *explore times they need help to be brave.*	*Quick Step* **"A Scary Day"**	• *Resources* CD	• CD player
	Option Times to Be Brave	• none	• white board, dry-erase marker
	Option Story from *Weekly Bible Reader®*	• *Weekly Bible Reader®* Issue 2	• none
Step 4 **Live It Out** Use one of these activities to help children *name a time they will ask for God's help to be brave.*	*Quick Step* **When You Ask for God's Help**	• *Activities* pp. 5 and 6	• markers or colored pencils
	Option Pass the Bag	• *Resources* CD	• 5 stones, paper lunch bag, CD player
	Saying Good-bye	• *Weekly Bible Reader®* Issue 2	• none

Life Focus
⊠ God helps us be brave.

Step 1 • Use one of these activities to help children **define what it means to be brave.** Use the Bible Memory activity to introduce the memory verses.

Welcome
- Welcome each child by name.
- Do check-in procedures you follow (name and security tags, offering, attendance chart, etc.).
- Early arrivers will enjoy doing one or more of the activities described on page 6.

≡ *Quick Step* Bravery Jump Up

Let's think about what it means to be brave. Tell the children that you will read several sentences. If a sentence describes someone being brave, they are to jump up and then sit down.

The firefighter rescued the family from the burning house.

Alex hid when it was time to go to the doctor.

Sarah told her friends about God even though they laughed at her.

Michael did not cry during the terrible storm.

Maria refused to go to bed because she was afraid of the dark.

Dylan and his family moved, and Dylan went to a new Sunday school class without complaining or crying.

Ethan told his mom the truth about breaking the window.

• **What does it mean to be brave?** (to have courage to do things even though you are afraid or don't know what might happen)

• **When are some times you have been brave?**

There are many times when we need to be brave. We're going to learn that ⊠ God helps us be brave.

Materials
none

Added Fun!
Let kids make up situations to tell the rest of the class.

Option Being Brave

Let's think about what it means to be brave as we do a fun activity. Put the children in pairs or small groups. Give each group one of the photo cards and a corresponding question to discuss and be ready to answer when called upon.

Soldier—How does a soldier show he is brave?

Doctor—How can you be brave when you go to the doctor?

Boy—How can the boy be brave when telling others about Jesus?

Firefighter—How do firefighters show they are brave?

Lightning—How can you be brave during a bad storm?

Girl—How can the girl be brave when she is alone?

• **What does it mean to be brave?** (to have courage to do things even though you are afraid or don't know what might happen)

There are many times when we need to be brave. We're going to learn that ⊠ God helps us be brave.

Materials
Resources Sheet 3
Lesson 2 photo cards

Bible Memory Psalms 124:8; 146:5

When you were only a baby, did you need help eating? (Invite all children to respond.) **Do you need help eating now? When you were a preschooler, did you need help getting dressed? Do you need help getting dressed now? When I was much younger, I needed help getting from place to place. But I don't need help anymore because I can drive a car. We all need help.** Read aloud Psalms 124:8 and 146:5. **According to these Bible verses, who helps us?** (the Lord) **Last week we learned that God helps us do our jobs. This week we're going to learn that ⊠ God helps us be brave.**

Materials
Bible

Transition to Explore His Word
See the *Resources* CD Transition Tips printable file. As children gather, make sure you have all the materials you need.

Explore His Word (20 minutes)

Step 2 • Use all of these activities to help children **describe a time God helped David be brave** and develop Bible skills.

Bible Background for the Teacher

The Philistine and Israelite armies had camped opposite each other, ready for war. For 40 days the Philistine giant named Goliath had taunted the Israelites to send out a soldier to fight him. In ancient times a one-on-one battle was sometimes conducted instead of a full-fledged war. Such a practice kept both armies from sustaining heavy casualties and some believed the outcome to be the result of the winner's god's intervention. With a 9-foot-plus "giant" on their team, it's no wonder the Philistines preferred this method of battle!

Besides his huge size, Goliath wore a bronze coat of armor that weighed 125 pounds and wore a bronze helmet on his head. He carried a huge javelin that had an iron point weighing 15 pounds and an armor-bearer walked in front of him.

David wanted to fight Goliath, but David had to overcome some obstacles—the Israelite army's fear, his oldest brother's insults, and Saul's discouragement. Evidently Goliath felt so much disdain for this shepherd boy coming to fight him in the name of the Lord that Goliath didn't even close the visor of his helmet.

Worship Time

If you want to offer a time of worship, see the *Resources* CD Worship Time Ideas printable file for suggestions.

Materials

white board, dry-erase marker, Bibles, book about David begun in Lesson 1, *Resources* Sheet 2 David name card and figures 2a–2f, 3 sheets of construction paper, reusable adhesive, *Teaching Picture* 2

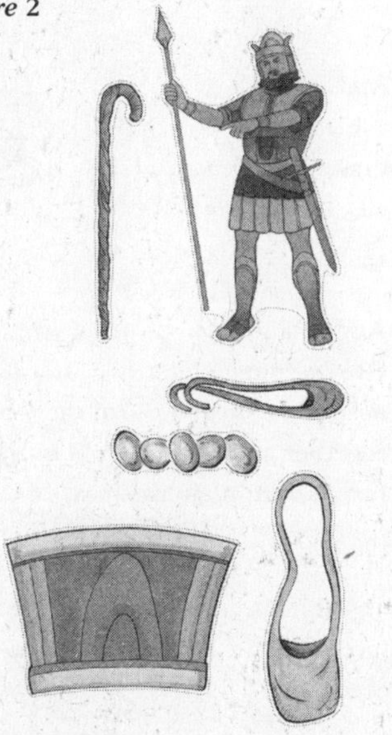

David Is Brave   (1 Samuel 17:1-52)

Our Bible story comes from the book of 1 Samuel. The Bible is divided into two main sections, the Old Testament and the New Testament. Write "1 Samuel 17:4" on the board. **Do you think 1 Samuel is in the Old Testament or New Testament?** (Old) Help children find 1 Samuel 17:4 in their Bibles. Ask for a volunteer to read the first part of the verse.

Choose a child to hold up the "David" name card whenever David's name is mentioned during the story. At the appropriate times, attach the figures with reusable adhesive to separate sheets of construction paper. Hold up the book about David begun in Lesson 1 and show the pages. **David was a shepherd who took care of sheep. David one time killed a bear to save his sheep and one time killed a lion to save his sheep.**

We're going to hear more about the life of David. Listen for a time God helped David be brave. Every time I say *Goliath*, **you say, "He was tall." Every time I say** *David,* **you say, "He was small."** Cue the children as needed.

The Israelite army, under the command of King Saul *(attach 2a to a sheet of paper)*, was preparing to do battle with the Philistine army. One of the Philistine soldiers was named **Goliath**. *(Attach 2b to a sheet of paper.)* **Goliath** was over 9 feet tall. He wore a bronze helmet on his head, and he wore lots of armor.

Goliath shouted to the Israelite army, "Are you coming to do battle with me? Choose one of your soldiers to fight me. If he kills me, the Philistines will become your servants. But if I kill the soldier you send to fight me, all you Israelites will become our servants." **Goliath's** words made King Saul *(show the crown)* and the entire army of Israel very afraid.

A man named Jesse had eight sons. The three oldest sons had joined the Israelite army. Jesse sent the youngest son, **David,** to take food to the three sons in the army and to find out if they were OK.

David reached the Israelite army and his brothers just as the Israelite army was going out to take up their battle positions. Then **Goliath** *(show 2b)* stepped out and shouted the same things as before. But no soldier from the Israelite army was brave enough to fight **Goliath**. They were terrified of him.

David asked, "Who is this that speaks against God? Who is this Philistine?" King Saul heard what **David** had said and sent for **David**. **David** told the king, "I will fight Goliath!"

David said to King Saul, "When a lion and a bear attacked the sheep I watch, God helped me kill them. Now God will help me defeat **Goliath**."

King Saul wanted **David** to wear his armor, but it was too big and heavy. So **David** set off to fight **Goliath** with only a staff in his hand, five smooth stones in a pouch, and a sling. *(Attach 2c, 2d, 2e, and 2f to a sheet of paper.)*

Goliath saw **David** coming toward him. **Goliath** made fun of him and taunted him—**David** was only a young man! But **David** said to **Goliath**, "You come against me with sword and spear and javelin, but I come against you in the name of the Lord Almighty, the God of the armies of Israel, whom you have defied" (17:45). "The battle is the Lord's and he will give all of you into our hands.'"

David ran to meet **Goliath**. **David** reached into his pouch, took out a stone, and put it in his sling. *(Show* Teaching Picture *2.)* He slung the stone, and it struck **Goliath** in the forehead. **Goliath** fell facedown. *(Drop the page with 2b to the floor.)* With God's help and a sling and a stone, **David** had killed **Goliath**! The Philistine army turned and ran. God had helped **David** be brave.

Bible Review Activity

When did God help David be brave? (when David went up against Goliath) **Let's see what else you remember from the story.** Distribute the activity pages and markers. Read the directions aloud. After kids have written the name of David on the blank line, they can cut on the cutting lines. Then help them fold the page accordion-style. Tell the children to open the pages so they can see Goliath.

• **How tall was Goliath?** (over 9 feet)
• **Why didn't anyone from the Israelite army want to fight Goliath?** (Goliath wore lots of armor. The soldiers were afraid of him.)
• **What did David take to fight Goliath?** (five stones, a sling)
• **Why did Goliath make fun of David?** (David was only a boy.)
• **What happened to Goliath?** (He fell facedown and died.)

God had helped David be brave and defeat Goliath! We're learning that ⊠ God helps us be brave too! Note: The back of this activity page will be used in Step 4.

Bible Skill Builder and Bible Memory Activity

Hold up a Bible. **The Bible is divided into two main sections. What are those two sections?** (Old and New Testament) **Which section tells about God making the world?** (Old) **Which section tells about Jesus being born?** (New) Write "Psalm 124:8" and "Psalm 146:5" on the board. **The book of Psalms is in the Old Testament.** Have children look in the table of contents in the front of their Bibles. Help them find the book of Psalms in the Old Testament section. Help children find the two memory verses and ask for volunteers to read the verses.

Play "Happy Are Those." Play again and invite kids to join in singing. The children will enjoy doing these motions while singing the song: *help*—one hand lifts the other hand up; *Lord*—make a capital *L* with the right hand thumb and index finger and bring that hand from the left shoulder to the right side of the waist; *Heaven*—spread both arms upward; *earth*—spread both arms downward; *happy*—move an open hand up the chest toward the neck.

We can be happy because God helps us. Just like David, ⊠ God helps us be brave.

Life Focus
⊠ God helps us be brave.

Special Note
Be sure to add the pages made today to the back of the book about David.

Materials
Activities p. 5, markers, scissors

Teaching Tip
For more questions, see the Review Questions on the *Resources* CD.

Materials
Bibles, white board, dry-erase marker, *Resources* CD Tracks 1 and 2, CD player

Added Fun!
Use the Bible Memory poster from *Resources* Sheet 1. Read the words together and have kids fill in the blanks with the missing words.

Make It Real (15 minutes)

Step 3 • Use one of these activities to help children **explore times they need help to be brave.**

Materials
Resources CD Track 8, CD player

≡ *Quick Step* "A Scary Day"

We've learned that God helped David be brave when David went up against Goliath. Let's explore times we need help to be brave as we listen to a story about Abby and her older brother Matt. Play the story and encourage the children to listen carefully. After the story ask these questions:

• **When were times Matt and Abby needed help to be brave?** (when they were afraid they would not be able to find their dog, when they were afraid of the storm)

• **What could Matt and Abby have done when they needed to be brave?** (They could have prayed and asked for God's help.)

Play the story again and let kids have fun making sound effects for the words *dog, wind, rain,* and *thunder.*

• **When are some times you need help to be brave?** (going to the doctor, during a bad storm, doing the right thing when no one else does, moving to a new place, being alone in the dark, going to a new school or church)

There are lots of times we need help to be brave. I'm glad that ⊠ God helps us be brave!

Materials
white board, dry-erase marker

Option   Times to Be Brave

We've learned that God helped David be brave when David went up against Goliath. Let's explore times we need help to be brave. Ask the children to name times they need help to be brave and write their responses on the board. (going to the doctor, during a bad storm, doing the right thing when no one else does, moving to a new place, being alone in the dark, going to a new school or church)

Divide the class into small groups. Tell the children that you will quietly tell each group one of the situations written on the board to act out. Give the groups a few minutes to decide how to act out the situations. As each group acts out its situation, the other children should guess what they are doing. Ask the following questions after each situation:

• **What makes it hard to be brave in this situation?**

• **Who can help you be brave in this situation?** (God)

There are lots of times we need help to be brave. I'm glad that ⊠ God helps us be brave!

Materials
Weekly Bible Reader®
Issue 2

Option   Story from *Weekly Bible Reader*®

We've learned that God helped David be brave when David went up against Goliath. Let's explore times we need help to be brave as we listen to a story. Read "Luis and Grandpa."

• **When are some times you need help to be brave?** (going to the doctor, during a bad storm, doing the right thing when no one else does, moving to a new place, being alone in the dark, going to a new school or church)

There are lots of times we need help to be brave. I'm glad that ⊠ God helps us be brave!

Life Focus
❤ God helps us be brave.

Step 4 • Use one of these activities to help children **name a time they will ask for God's help to be brave.**

Quick Step   When You Ask for God's Help

We've learned that God helped David be brave. And we know that there are lots of times we need help to be brave. Be thinking of a time you will ask for God's help to be brave. If you did not have the children do the activity from *Activities* page 5 in Step 2, they can do it now. (See the directions in the Step 2 Bible Review Activity.) Have kids turn their Goliath pictures over. Read the words in the first column and have kids write "me" on the blank line. Then read the words in the second column. Tell kids to write or draw a picture of a time they will ask for God's help to be brave. They can also color the outline letters.

Have the children fold the page, accordion-style, on the fold lines. Say this rhyme: **When you need help to be brave, you may feel very small.** Ask the kids to unfold the page. **But when you ask for God's help, you won't feel small at all!** Have the kids fold the page. Say the rhyme again, inviting children to join you in saying the rhyme as they unfold the page.

Close with a time of prayer. Encourage children to pray and ask for God's help to be brave.

Materials
Activities pp. 5 and 6, markers or colored pencils

Option   Pass the Bag

We've learned that God helped David be brave. And we know that there are lots of times we need help to be brave. Be thinking of a time you will ask for God's help to be brave as we play a fun game. Before class, put five small stones in a paper lunch bag. Have the children sit or stand in a circle. Show children the bag containing the five stones. Tell the kids to pass the bag while playing "Happy Are Those." Whoever is holding the bag when the music stops can name a time she will ask for God's help to be brave. Continue playing until all the children have had a turn to name a time when they will ask for God's help to be brave.

Ask the children to remain in a circle for the prayer time. Encourage children to pray and ask for God's help to be brave.

Materials
5 stones, paper lunch bag, *Resources* CD Tracks 1 and 2, CD player

Added Fun!
Give each child a paper lunch bag containing five small stones. Tell the children that the stones can be a reminder to ask for God's help to be brave.

Saying Good-bye
- Distribute Issue 2 of *Weekly Bible Reader.*®
- Make sure children have projects and activity sheets they have done.
- If you have time before parents arrive, use some of the activities on page 6.
- Remind parents that a weekly *Faith & Family* page is available online to print and use with their child at home. Go to heartshaper.com.

Evaluate
- In what ways did the children show their understanding that God will help them be brave?
- How did you demonstrate care and concern for the children in your class?

David and Jonathan Are Friends

Bible Focus: 1 Samuel 18:1-15; 19:1-10; 20:42
Bible Memory: Our help is in the name of the LORD, the Maker of heaven and earth (Psalm 124:8). Blessed are those whose help is the God of Jacob, whose hope is in the LORD their God (Psalm 146:5).
Life Focus: ▨ God helps us be friends.

Heart to Heart

It's great to have friends! God gave David a friend named Jonathan at just the right time to help David through a particularly difficult time in his life. Jonathan encouraged David and supported him even when it wasn't easy.

You can find encouragement by reminding yourself of those friends God has placed in your life to help you through difficult times. Thank God for friends who encourage and support you even when it isn't easy. And ask God to let you be a friend to others as Jonathan was to David. Encourage and help friends at just the right time, offering lots of support and love.

Lesson 3 at a Glance

		HeartShaper Materials	Other Materials
Step 1 **Focus In** Use one of these activities to help children *explore being a friend.*	*Quick Step* **What Is a Friend?** *Activity Page*	• *Activities* p. 7 and corresponding stickers	• pencils
	Option Colors of Friendship *Action*	• none	• construction paper
	Bible Memory *Use this activity to introduce the Bible Memory verses.* *Music*	• *Resources* CD	• Bible, CD player
Step 2 **Explore His Word** Use all of these activities to help children *tell how God helped Jonathan be a friend to David* and develop Bible skills.	**David and Jonathan Are Friends** *Bible Story*	• *Resources* Sheet 2 David name card, Sheet 1 figures 3a–3e and Bible Memory poster, CD Review Questions Unit 1 printable file; *Teaching Picture* 3; book about David used in Lessons 1 and 2; *Activities* p. 8	• white board, dry-erase marker, Bibles, paper plates or paper, markers, construction paper, reusable adhesive, markers or pencils
	Bible Review Activity *Activity Page*		
	Bible Skill Builder and Bible Memory Activity *Bible Skills*		
Step 3 **Make It Real** Use one of these activities to help children *identify reasons to be friends with others.*	*Quick Step* **Thumbs-up or Down** *Action*	• none	• none
	Option Friendship Bridge *Music*	• none	• none
	Option Story from *Weekly Bible Reader®* *Listen*	• *Weekly Bible Reader®* Issue 3	• none
Step 4 **Live It Out** Use one of these activities to help children *practice being a friend.*	*Quick Step* **Friendly Role Plays** *Act It Out*	• none	• paper, marker, container or basket
	Option Friendly Cards *Art*	• reproducible p. 90	• scissors, markers
	Saying Good-bye	• *Weekly Bible Reader®* Issue 3	• none

Focus In (15 minutes)

Step 1 • Use one of these activities to help children **explore being a friend.**
Use the Bible Memory activity to introduce the memory verses.

Welcome
- Welcome each child by name.
- Do check-in procedures you follow (name and security tags, offering, attendance chart, etc.).
- Early arrivers will enjoy doing one or more of the activities described on page 6.

Quick Step   What Is a Friend?

Let's think about what it means to be a friend. Distribute the activity pages, stickers, and pencils. Read the directions aloud and do the page together. (The stickers in order are: That's OK. I forgive you. I hope you're better soon. You're fun to be with. You're so kind. I'll help you. The words in order are: forgiving, caring, fun, kind, helpful. The sentence at the end: I will be a <u>friend</u>.)
- **What are some things you can do to be a friend to others?** (be nice, share toys, forgive, help, pray for others, say nice things)
- **Tell about something a friend has done for you.**

There are lots of ways to be a friend to others. We're going to learn that ⊠ God helps us be friends.

Materials
Activities p. 7 and corresponding stickers, pencils

Option   Colors of Friendship

Let's think about what it means to be a friend as we do a fun activity. Give each child one sheet of construction paper. When you call out one of the colors of paper, the kids holding that color can stand up and respond to the question. Encourage the children to not repeat what someone else has said.

Red—**What is something kind a friend might say to you?**
Blue—**What is something a friend might help you with?**
Yellow—**What is something fun that friends can do together?**
Green—**What is a way a friend can help when someone is sick?**
- **What are some things you do to be a friend to others?**

There are lots of ways to be a friend to others. We're going to learn that ⊠ God helps us be friends.

Materials
construction paper
(red, blue, yellow, green)

Added Fun!
Let kids make up questions about being a friend to ask the rest of the class.

Bible Memory   Psalms 124:8; 146:5

Listen to these verses of Scripture to find out what the Lord made. Read aloud Psalms 124:8 and 146:5. **What did the Lord make?** (Heaven and earth) **What else did the Lord God make?** Encourage all children to name something God made. **God made everything! The Lord God, the maker of everything, is the one who can help us.** Play "Happy Are Those" and invite children to join in singing. Motions for the song can be found on page 16. **God helps us in lots of ways. We've learned that God helps us do our jobs and that God helps us be brave. This week we're going to learn that ⊠ God helps us be friends.**

Materials
Bible, *Resources* CD Tracks 1 and 2, CD player

Transition to Explore His Word
See the *Resources* CD Transition Tips printable file. As children gather, make sure you have all the materials you need.

Explore His Word (20 minutes)

Step 2 • Use all of these activities to help children **tell how God helped Jonathan be a friend to David** and develop Bible skills.

Bible Background for the Teacher

After defeating the Philistine giant Goliath, the whole country of Israel was singing the praises of David, including King Saul and his son Jonathan, who emotionally bonded with David. At Saul's request David moved into the palace. Jonathan and David swore an oath of friendship to each other. Jonathan's giving of his robe, tunic, sword, bow, and belt to David was an affectionate act of friendship and may have symbolized Prince Jonathan's acknowledgment and acceptance of David as Israel's next king.

Saul began giving David more military assignments, which David successfully completed. The country continued to praise David but at the expense of King Saul's ego. This sparked the beginning of Saul's numerous attempts to kill David, including several times when Saul openly hurled his sword at David. Some of Saul's attempts were more discreet, such as sending David into battles that were likely to end David's life.

Jonathan, even at the risk of his own life, spoke to his irrational father and interceded for David on a number of occasions. Jonathan also kept David informed of Saul's murderous plots. In the end a heartbroken Jonathan assisted David in fleeing Saul's presence (1 Samuel 20). Years later, even after Jonathan's death, David would continue to honor his oath of friendship by caring for Jonathan's son, Mephibosheth, who was disabled (2 Samuel 9).

Worship Time

If you want to offer a time of worship, see the *Resources* CD Worship Time Ideas printable file for suggestions.

Materials

white board; dry-erase marker; Bibles; paper plates or paper; markers; book about David used in Lessons 1 and 2; *Resources* Sheet 2 David name card, Sheet 1 figures 3a–3e; 3 sheets of construction paper; reusable adhesive; *Teaching Picture* 3

David and Jonathan Are Friends   (1 Samuel 18:1-15; 19:1-10; 20:42)

Our Bible story comes from the book of 1 Samuel. Write "Old Testament," "New Testament," and "1 Samuel 18:1" on the board. **Do you think that the book of 1 Samuel is in the Old Testament or the New Testament?** (Old) Help children find 1 Samuel 18:1 in their Bibles. Ask for a volunteer to read the verse.

Give each child a paper plate or sheet of paper and a marker. Tell kids to draw a happy face on one side and a sad face on the other side. Choose a child to hold the "David" name card during the story. Ask that child to hold up the name card whenever David's name is mentioned. At the appropriate times, attach the figures with reusable adhesive to separate sheets of construction paper.

Hold up the book about David used in Lessons 1 and 2 and show the pages. **David was a shepherd who took care of sheep. David one time killed a bear to save his sheep and one time killed a lion to save his sheep. A little while after this, David then went up against the very tall Goliath with only a staff, five stones, and a sling. God helped David be brave and kill Goliath.**

We're going to hear more about the life of David. There are some happy events in this story and some sad events. When you hear about a happy event, hold up the happy face. When you hear about a sad event, hold up the sad face. Cue the children as needed. **And you need to listen for a time God helped a young man named Jonathan be a friend to David.**

After **David** had killed Goliath, **David** went to live with King Saul. That's when Jonathan and **David** became friends. *(Kids show happy faces.)* Jonathan was King Saul's son. Jonathan said, "I love you, **David**. Let's be friends." *(Show Teaching Picture 3.)* Jonathan loved **David** so much that he gave him a robe, a tunic, a sword, a bow, and a belt. *(Attach 3a, 3b, and 3c to a sheet of paper.)*

King Saul sent **David** to fight in other battles. He even put **David** in charge of other soldiers. Every time King Saul gave **David** a job to do, **David** did the job well. *(happy faces)*

Life Focus
⊠ God helps us be friends.

When King Saul, **David**, and the army were returning from battle, women greeted them and sang about their victories. *(happy faces)* They sang that Saul had killed thousands but **David** had killed tens of thousands. This made Saul angry. He was king! King Saul became jealous of **David**. *(sad faces)*

One day **David** was playing his harp for King Saul. *(Attach 3d to a sheet of paper.)* All of a sudden, King Saul picked up his spear and threw it at **David**. *(Attach 3e to a sheet of paper; sad faces.)* **David** jumped aside just in time. The king threw the spear again. *(sad faces)* But that spear didn't hit **David** either.

Everything **David** did was successful because God was with him. *(happy faces)* All the people loved **David** too. This made Saul even more jealous of **David**. King Saul kept trying to kill **David**. *(sad faces)* He sent **David** into battles where he thought **David** would be killed. He told his servants, and even his son Jonathan, to kill **David**. But Jonathan was **David's** friend. *(happy faces)*

Jonathan said, "**David**, be on the lookout for danger. My father is trying to kill you." Jonathan even talked to his father to try to convince him not to kill **David**. But one day **David** was playing the harp for King Saul when Saul again tried to kill **David** with a spear. *(sad faces)* That's when **David** ran away.

But Jonathan was still **David's** friend. *(happy faces)* **David** and Jonathan said, "We promise that we will always be friends." And they were. **David** was glad God had given him such a good friend as Jonathan.

Special Note
Be sure to add the pages made today to the back of the book about David.

Bible Review Activity

How did God help Jonathan be a friend to David? (Jonathan gave David his robe, tunic, sword, bow, and belt. Jonathan warned David that his father was trying to kill David. Jonathan tried to convince his father not to kill David. Jonathan promised to always be friends with David.) **Let's see what else you remember from the Bible story.** Distribute the activity pages and markers or pencils. Read the directions aloud and do the page together.

As time permits, play a fun review game. Have the children sit or stand in a circle. Have kids pass figure 3a around the circle until you say "David and Jonathan!" Ask the child holding the figure a question about the story using the Review Questions.

God helped Jonathan be a good friend to David. We're learning that ⊠ God helps us be friends too!

Materials
Activities p. 8; markers or pencils; *Resources* Sheet 1 figure 3a, CD Review Questions Unit 1 for Lesson 3 printable file

Bible Skill Builder and Bible Memory Activity

Hold up a Bible. **Into what two main sections is the Bible divided?** (Old and New Testaments) **What does the Old Testament tell about?** (God making the world) **What does the New Testament tell about?** (Jesus being born) Write "Psalm 124:8" and "Psalm 146:5" on the board. **The book of Psalms is in the Old Testament.** Have children look in the table of contents in the front of their Bibles. Help them find the Old Testament section and tell them to run their fingers down the list until they see the book of Psalms. Help children find the two memory verses and ask for volunteers to read the verses.

Display the Bible Memory poster. If you previously used the poster, remove the press-out words from the verses. Read the words while pointing to them. Pause when you come to an empty space and ask who knows what word is missing. When a child says the right word, let him attach it to the poster with reusable adhesive. When all the spaces have been filled, lead the kids in saying together the memory verses.

It's great to know that God helps us. ⊠ God helps us be friends with others just like Jonathan was a good friend to David.

Materials
Bibles, white board, dry-erase marker, *Resources* Sheet 1 Bible Memory poster, reusable adhesive

Teaching Tip
Print and use the Unit 1 Bible Skills Worksheets found on the *Resources* CD to help children know that the Bible has an Old Testament and a New Testament and to understand the basic differences between them.

Make It Real (15 minutes)

Step 3 • Use one of these activities to help children **identify reasons to be friends with others.**

Materials
none

Expert Tip
"I've found that the more time I spend preparing my lessons, the less time I end up lecturing, yet, the more the children end up learning!"
—*Steven James*

≡ *Quick Step* Thumbs-up or Down
We've learned that God helped Jonathan be a good friend to David. Let's explore reasons we should be friends with others. Tell the children that you will read several sentences. If a sentence gives a good reason to be friends with others, they should show two thumbs-up. If a sentence does not give a good reason to be friends with others, they should show two thumbs-down.

You should be friends so you'll get invited to lots of parties. (down)
You should be friends and help others because God helps you. (up)
You should be friends so you will be popular. (down)
You should be friends *only* because it will make you feel good. (down)
You should be friends so you can tell them about Jesus. (up)
You should be friends so they will give you new clothes. (down)
You should be friends so they will give you lots of birthday presents. (down)
You should be friends because God wants you to be friends. (up)

There are lots of good reasons to be friends with others. And remember that you don't have to do it on your own. ☒ God helps us be friends!

Materials
none

Option Friendship Bridge
We've learned that God helped Jonathan be a friend to David. What are some good reasons we should be friends with others? (God wants us to be friends with others. So we can tell them about Jesus. We can help others and be their friends because God helps us. When we are friends with others, they will usually be friends with us.)

Ask two children to form a bridge with clasped hands and raised arms for others to walk under. Invite the children to join in singing the following words to the tune of "London Bridge" while walking around the room and under the bridge: **God helps us to be good friends, good friends, good friends. God helps us to be good friends. Thank You, God!** When the song is done, tell the two children to lower the bridge. Whoever is caught in the bridge needs to tell a good reason to be friends with others. Be sure that each child gets a turn.

There are lots of good reasons to be friends with others. And remember that you don't have to do it on your own. ☒ God helps us be friends!

Materials
Weekly Bible Reader®
Issue 3

Option Story from *Weekly Bible Reader®*
We've learned that God helped Jonathan be a good friend to David. Let's explore reasons we should be friends with others as we listen to a story. Read "Dante's Friend."

• **What are some good reasons we should be friends with others?** (God wants us to be friends with others. So we can tell them about Jesus. We can help others and be their friends because God helps us. When we are friends with others, they will usually be friends with us.)

There are lots of good reasons to be friends with others. And remember that you don't have to do it on your own. ☒ God helps us be friends!

Step 4 • Use one of these activities to help children **practice being a friend.**

≡ *Quick Step* Friendly Role Plays

We've learned that God helped Jonathan be a good friend to David. And we've identified some good reasons we should be friends with others. We know ❤ **God helps us be friends, so we're going to practice being a friend.** Before class, write the following on separate slips of paper and put in a container or basket: help with homework, make something for a sick friend, share a toy, invite someone to play with you, share a cookie, let a friend go first in line, say kind things, say hello to a new child in class, and so forth.

Ask for a volunteer to choose a slip of paper. Guide the child to act out the way of being a friend described on the paper. Allow the child to choose a friend or two as needed to help in doing the role play. Invite the rest of the class to guess what the child is acting out. Continue until every child has participated. Remind the children that ❤ God helps us be friends!

Close with a time of prayer. Encourage all children to pray and thank God for friends and ask God to help them be good friends to others.

Materials
paper, marker, container or basket

Teaching Tip
Providing simple props can help young children act out situations.

Option   Friendly Cards

We've learned that God helped Jonathan be a good friend to David. And we've identified some good reasons we should be friends with others. We know ❤ **God helps us be friends, so we're going to practice being a friend by making a card to give to a friend.** Before class, make copies of the reproducible page. Give children copies of the reproducible page. Ask for a volunteer to read the words on the front of the card. Then direct the kids to cut out the hearts and help them to fold on the fold lines. Let them write friendly messages inside, color, and decorate the cards. You may want to provide some colorful stickers for the children to add also. While children work on the cards, ask them to share the name of the friends they plan on giving their cards to.

Close with a time of prayer. Ask for several volunteers to pray and thank God for their friends. Also ask for several volunteers to ask God for His help in being good friends to others.

Materials
reproducible p. 90, scissors, markers
(optional: stickers)

Teaching Tip
Copying the card onto card stock will make it more durable.

Saying Good-bye

- Distribute Issue 3 of *Weekly Bible Reader.*®
- Make sure children have projects and activity sheets they have done.
- If you have time before parents arrive, use some of the activities on page 6.
- Remind parents that a weekly *Faith & Family* page is available online to print and use with their child at home. Go to heartshaper.com.

Evaluate
- How did the children demonstrate that they are understanding more about the help that God gives us?
- Which children are not comfortable praying aloud? How can you help them?

David Does the Right Thing

Bible Focus: 1 Samuel 26
Bible Memory: Our help is in the name of the LORD, the Maker of heaven and earth (Psalm 124:8). Blessed are those whose help is the God of Jacob, whose hope is in the LORD their God (Psalm 146:5).
Life Focus: ⊠ God helps us do right things.

Heart to Heart

David had the opportunity to take revenge on King Saul. But David knew that this was not God's way of handling the situation and God helped David do the right thing. The next time you have a choice to either lie or tell the truth, be like David and do the right thing. The next time you have a choice to either be rude or be kind to a family member, be like David and do the right thing. The next time you have a choice to either be patient with the kids in your class or not be patient with them, be like David and do the right thing. Ask for God's help in doing right things.

Lesson 4 at a Glance

Step 1		HeartShaper Materials	Other Materials
Focus In Use one of these activities to help children *explore doing right and wrong things.*	*Quick Step* **Cody's Story** (LISTEN)	• none	• none
	Option Right and Wrong Toss (Action)	• none	• poster board, marker, beanbag
	Bible Memory *Use this activity to introduce the Bible Memory verses.* (Memorize)	• *Resources* Sheet 1 Bible Memory poster	• Bible, reusable adhesive

Step 2			
Explore His Word Use all of these activities to help children *describe a time God helped David do the right thing* and develop Bible skills.	**David Does the Right Thing** (Bible Story)	• *Resources* Sheet 2 David name card, Sheet 1 figures 4a and 4b, CD; book about David from Lessons 1–3, *Teaching Picture* 4	• white board, dry-erase marker, Bibles, construction paper, reusable adhesive, CD player
	Bible Review Activity (Action)		
	Bible Skill Builder and Bible Memory Activity (Bible Skills)		

Step 3			
Make It Real Use one of these activities to help children *discover reasons they need to do right things.*	*Quick Step* **Doing Right Things** (Activity Page)	• *Activities* p. 9	• scissors, glue
	Option Kids Doing Right (DISCUSS)	• *Resources* Sheet 3 Lesson 4 photo cards	• none
	Option Story from *Weekly Bible Reader®* (LISTEN)	• *Weekly Bible Reader®* Issue 4	• none

Step 4			
Live It Out Use one of these activities to help children *plan ways to do right things.*	*Quick Step* **Doing Right Game** (Game)	• *Resources* CD	• CD player
	Option Planning to Do Right Things (Craft)	• *Activities* p. 9	• index cards or paper, markers, plastic or paper cups, clear tape
	Saying Good-bye	• *Weekly Bible Reader®* Issue 4	• none

Life Focus
⊠ God helps us do right things.

Step 1 • Use one of these activities to help children **explore doing right and wrong things.**
Use the Bible Memory activity to introduce the memory verses.

Welcome
- Welcome each child by name.
- Do check-in procedures you follow (name and security tags, offering, attendance chart, etc.).
- Early arrivers will enjoy doing one or more of the activities described on page 6.

▤ *Quick Step* Cody's Story

Let's explore doing right and wrong things. Tell the children that you will tell them about a boy named Cody. When they hear something right that Cody did, they should clap their hands. When they hear something wrong that he did, they should snap their fingers.

Cody didn't get out of bed when his mother asked him to. (snap) **Cody thanked his mom for making pancakes.** (clap) **On the school bus Cody was nice to a new kid.** (clap) **Cody ran in the hallway at school.** (snap) **Cody had studied hard for the spelling test.** (clap) **Cody told his teacher that his dog ate his homework.** (snap) **Cody cleaned his room without his dad asking him to do it.** (clap) **Cody prayed and thanked God for a good day.** (clap)

- **What are some other wrong things we do?**
- **What are some other right things we do?**

Just like Cody, there are lots of right things and wrong things we do. We're going to learn that ⊠ God helps us do right things.

Materials
none

Added Fun!
Ask for volunteers to make up stories about doing right and wrong things.

Option   Right and Wrong Toss

Let's think about doing right and wrong things. Before class, make a grid of 12 spaces on a piece of poster board. In each grid write one of the following: share, lie, worship God, steal, be a good friend, talk back to parents, obey teachers, don't obey parents, work hard, keep promises, be mean to others, be kind.

Lay the poster board on the floor. Let the kids take turns tossing the beanbag onto the poster board. The children are to read the words where the beanbag lands and say whether that is a right or wrong thing to do. After everyone has had a turn, play again. This time, when the beanbag lands on a wrong thing to do, have the children say what the right thing to do would be.

- **What are some other wrong things to do?**
- **What are some other right things to do?**

There are many right things we can do and many wrong things we can do too. We're going to learn that ⊠ God helps us do right things.

Materials
poster board, marker, beanbag

Teaching Tip
If you have a large class, make several grids.

Bible Memory   Psalms 124:8; 146:5

Read aloud Psalms 124:8 and 146:5. **Our Bible Memory verses tell us that our help comes from whom?** (the Lord God) Display the Bible Memory poster. Lead the kids in reading the verses. Guide them to attach with reusable adhesive the missing words and picture in the right spaces. When all the spaces have been filled, lead the kids in saying together the memory verses. **We've learned that God helps us do our jobs, helps us be brave, and helps us be friends. This week we're going to learn that ⊠ God helps us do right things.**

Materials
Bible, *Resources* Sheet 1 Bible Memory poster, reusable adhesive

Transition to Explore His Word
See the *Resources* CD Transition Tips printable file. As children gather, make sure you have all the materials you need.

Explore His Word (20 minutes)

Step 2 • Use all of these activities to help children **describe a time God helped David do the right thing** and develop Bible skills.

Bible Background for the Teacher

David, admired for his defeat of Goliath and other military achievements, had gone from celebrity status to being a fugitive on the run. King Saul was jealous of David's popularity and recognized that God's intentions were for David to replace him as king. Therefore, Saul was chasing David around the countryside trying to kill him. The 3,000 soldiers with Saul were his standing army.

David found Saul and his army asleep in their camp. David could have read into the situation that it was God's will for him to kill Saul. David also could have given into the emotion of revenge and killed Saul, thus placing himself in a position to assume the throne.

Sparing King Saul's life, David took the king's spear and water jug as proof that David could have killed Saul. David had a strong conviction that Saul's kingship was established by God. So strong was that conviction that David later killed a man who claimed to have assisted in taking King Saul's life (2 Samuel 1:2-10). In his dealings with Saul, David always acted with integrity and did what was right.

Worship Time

If you want to offer a time of worship, see the *Resources* CD Worship Time Ideas printable file for suggestions.

Materials

white board; dry-erase marker; Bibles; book about David used in Lessons 1–3; *Resources* Sheet 2 David name card, Sheet 1 figures 4a and 4b; construction paper; reusable adhesive; *Teaching Picture* 4

Story Option

Play Track 9 from the *Resources* CD for a dramatization of the Bible story.

David Does the Right Thing   (1 Samuel 26)

Our Bible story comes from the book of 1 Samuel. Write "1 Samuel 26:2" on the board. **Is the book of 1 Samuel in the Old Testament or the New Testament?** (Old) Help children find 1 Samuel 26:2 in their Bibles. Ask for a volunteer to read the verse.

Choose a child to hold up the "David" name card whenever David's name is mentioned during the story. At the appropriate times, attach the figures with reusable adhesive to a sheet of construction paper. Hold up the book about David used in Lessons 1–3 and show the pages.

David was a shepherd who took care of sheep. David one time killed a bear to save his sheep and one time killed a lion to save his sheep. A little while after this, David then went up against the very tall Goliath with only a staff, five smooth stones in a pouch, and a sling. God helped David be brave and kill Goliath. Then God helped Jonathan be a good friend to David.

We're going to hear more about the life of David. When you hear the words *quietly, sleeping, whispered,* or *sleep,* hold a finger to your mouth. During the story, cue the children as needed. **And you need to listen for a time God helped David do the right thing.**

David had once lived with King Saul and played his harp for the king. King Saul would send **David** into battle. **David** was always successful because God was with him. When **David** returned from battles, people would cheer and praise him. But that made King Saul jealous of **David.** King Saul was so jealous he tried to kill **David** several times. That's when **David** ran away.

But King Saul chased **David,** searching for **David** in order to kill him. One day the king led 3,000 of his best soldiers to find **David. David** sent scouts to find out where the king and his soldiers were camped.

David and Abishai (Uh-bish-ay-eye) crept **quietly** into King Saul's camp. (*Show* Teaching Picture 4.) They saw that Saul and Abner, the commander of Saul's army, were **sleeping.** Saul's entire army was camped around them. Saul's spear was stuck in the ground by his head, and there was a jug of water beside him. (*Attach 4a and 4b to a sheet of paper.*)

Life Focus

☒ God helps us do right things.

Abishai **whispered** to **David**, "Now is your opportunity to get rid of Saul. Let me kill him."

But **David** said, "No! Don't kill him! God chose him to be the king. It wouldn't be right for me to kill him. Maybe he will die in some other way, but I will not kill him. Get Saul's spear and water jug, and let's go!" Saul and his men did not wake up because God had caused them to fall into a deep **sleep.**

When **David** and Abishai got some distance away, **David** called out to Abner, the commander of Saul's army. Abner didn't know who was calling. **David** said, "Why didn't you guard the king well last night? Where are the king's spear and water jug?" Saul heard the voice and wondered if it was **David.**

David answered, "Yes, it's **David**. Why are you searching for me, trying to kill me? What evil have I done?"

Saul replied, "I have been wrong. You could have killed me, but you didn't. I won't try to kill you again."

David told Saul to send someone after the king's spear and water jug. "I did the right thing by not killing you," said **David**. "I knew God chose you to be king. Now may God give me rest from my troubles."

Saul said, "May God bless you, **David**. You will do great things." Then Saul and his men returned home. **David** had done the right thing, and God blessed him.

Special Note

Be sure to add the pages made today to the back of the book about David begun in Lesson 1. See p. 9.

Bible Review Activity

How did God help David do the right thing? (God helped David not kill King Saul.) **Let's see what else you remember from the story.** Divide the class into two groups. Assign one group to be the "King Saul" group and one group to be the "David" group. Tell the children that you will ask questions about the story. If the answer is King Saul, that group should stand and say "King Saul!" If the answer is David, that group should stand and say "David!"

I played the harp. (David) **I was jealous of my son's friend.** (Saul) **God was with me.** (David) **I tried to kill my son's friend.** (Saul) **Abishai went with me to the king's camp.** (David) **I had an army of 3,000 men with me.** (Saul) **I had a spear and water jug close to me while I slept.** (Saul) **I would not kill the king.** (David) **I asked Abner why he hadn't guarded the king very well.** (David) **I asked why the king was trying to kill me.** (David) **I promised I wouldn't try to kill David again.** (Saul) **I did the right thing by not killing the king.** (David)

God helped David do the right thing. We're learning that ☒ **God helps us do right things too!**

Materials

none

Added Fun!

Hold up the book about David used in the Bible stories. Point to the items and have kids tell about them.

Bible Skill Builder and Bible Memory Activity

Hold up a Bible. **How many main sections does the Bible have?** (two) **What are these two main sections?** (Old Testament, New Testament) **What does the Old Testament tell about?** (God making the world) **What does the New Testament tell about?** (Jesus being born) Write "Psalm 124:8" and "Psalm 146:5" on the board. **Is the book of Psalms in the Old Testament or New Testament?** (Old) Have children look in the table of contents in the front of their Bibles. Help them find the Old Testament section and tell them to run their fingers down the list until they see the book of Psalms. Help children find the two memory verses and ask for volunteers to read the verses. Encourage children to say the verses from memory.

Play "Happy Are Those" and invite kids to join in singing. Motions can be found on page 16. **We can be happy because God helps us. Just like David,** ☒ **God helps us do right things.**

Materials

Bibles, white board, dry-erase marker, *Resources* CD Tracks 1 and 2, CD player

Teaching Tip

Print and use the Unit 1 Bible Skills Worksheets found on the *Resources* CD to help children know that the Bible has an Old Testament and a New Testament and to understand the basic differences between them.

Make It Real (15 minutes)

Step 3 • Use one of these activities to help children **discover reasons they need to do right things.**

Materials
Activities p. 9,
scissors, glue

Activity Page

Note
This activity page will also be used
in Step 4.

≡ *Quick Step* Doing Right Things

We've discovered that God helped David do the right thing by not kill-ing King Saul. Let's discover reasons why we need to do right things. Distribute the activity pages, scissors, and glue. Read the directions aloud. **Why do you think there is a water jug on this page?** (David took King Saul's water jug.) Guide the children to glue to the water jug only those sentences that tell reasons they need to do right things.

 • **Why is "I will get money for doing right things" not a good reason to do right things?**
 • **Why is "doing right things is always easy" not a good reason to do right things?**
 • **Why is "I will get candy for doing right things" not a good reason to do right things?**

There are lots of good reasons to do right things. And remember that you don't have to do it on your own. ☒ God helps us do right things!

Materials
Resources Sheet 3
Lesson 4 photo cards

DISCUSS

Teaching Tip
If you have a small class, give each
child one or two of the photo cards.

Option Kids Doing Right

We've learned that God helped David do the right thing by not killing King Saul. Let's discover reasons why we need to do right things. Put the children in pairs or small groups. Give each group one of the photo cards and tell groups to look at their photos. **These are all photos of kids doing right things. Decide what *will* happen because the kid in your photo is doing the right thing. Also decide what *could* happen if the kid in your photo *didn't* do the right thing.** Give the groups a few minutes and help only as needed. Let each group share. (Example: Because the girl is feeding the fish, it will stay healthy and not be hungry. If she didn't feed the fish it would be hun-gry and eventually die.)

 • **What are some other reasons you need to do right things?** (God wants me to do right things. Parents want me to do right things. Doing right things is best for others.)

There are lots of good reasons to do right things. And remember that you don't have to do it on your own. ☒ God helps us do right things!

Materials
Weekly Bible Reader®
Issue 4

LISTEN

Option Story from *Weekly Bible Reader®*

We've learned that God helped David do the right thing by not killing King Saul. Let's discover reasons why we need to do right things. Read "Ryan Does Right."

 • **What are some reasons you need to do right things?** (God wants me to do right things. Parents want me to do right things. Doing right things is best for others.)

There are lots of good reasons to do right things. And remember that you don't have to do it on your own. ☒ God helps us do right things!

Live It Out (10 minutes)

Step 4 • Use one of these activities to help children **plan ways to do right things.**

≡ *Quick Step* Doing Right Game

We've learned that God helped David do the right thing by not killing King Saul. And we've discovered reasons to do right things. We know ❤ God helps us do right things, so now you need to plan ways you will do right things. Have the children sit or stand in a circle. Say, **"A way I plan on doing right is ___."** Ask one of the children next to you to say, **"___ (your name) plans on doing right by ___. I plan on doing right by ___."** Keep going around the circle with the children saying what the previous children said and then adding how they plan on doing right.

Play "Show My Love." Invite kids to join in. Remind kids that we show our love to God when we choose to do right..

Close with prayer. Invite the children to pray the following prayer after you: **Dear God** (pause), **thank You for helping us** (pause). **Thank You for helping us do our jobs** (pause). **Thank You for helping us be brave** (pause). **Thank You for helping us be friends** (pause). **Thank You for helping us do right things** (pause). **In Jesus' name, amen.**

Materials
Resources CD Tracks 5 and 6, CD player

Option Planning to Do Right Things

We've learned that God helped David do the right thing by not killing King Saul. And we've discovered reasons to do right things. We know ❤ God helps us do right things, so now you need to plan ways you will do right things. If you did not have the children do the activity page in Step 3, have them do it now. Next give children several index cards or small pieces of paper. Ask them to write or draw on each card ways they plan on doing right things. Then give the children the cups and have them put their cards into the cups. Show the kids how to tape the cups to the backsides of their *Activities* water jug so that the jugs stand up.

Ask children to share ways they plan on doing right things. Tell kids to take their water jugs home and put them where they can see them often. They can pull from their cups a way to do a right thing each day and ask for God's help to do it.

Close with a time of prayer. Ask for volunteers to pray for God's help to do right things.

Materials
Activities p. 9, index cards or paper, markers, plastic or paper cups, clear tape

Saying Good-bye

• Distribute Issue 4 of *Weekly Bible Reader*® and the *Activities* page 2 Unit 1 Bible Memory poster and stickers if you have not already done so. You may also want to distribute the *Activities* Mystery Ink™ pages.

• Make sure children have projects and activity sheets they have done.

• If you have time before parents arrive, use some of the activities on page 6.

• Remind parents that a weekly *Faith & Family* page is available online to print and use with their child at home. Go to heartshaper.com.

Evaluate
• How willing are the children to do right things?
• How well did you give each child a listening ear and kind words?

Unit 2

Bible Memory

Psalm 86:9, 10

All the nations you have made will come and worship before you, Lord; they will bring glory to your name. For you are great and do marvelous deeds; you alone are God.

Print the KJV or NIV Additional Bible Memory file from the Resources CD for more Bible Memory verses kids will enjoy learning.

Bible Skill for Unit 2

Children will

- understand what a Scripture reference means.

Ongoing Bible Skills

Children will

- find verses in the Bible.
- begin to read Bible verses.
- memorize selected Bible verses.

Life Skills for Unit 2

Children will

- desire to worship and praise God.
- thank God for His care.
- choose to obey God's instructions.

	Bible Focus	Life Focus
Lesson 5 God Cares for Elijah	Ravens feed Elijah. 1 Kings 16, 17	☒ We can praise God because He cares for us.
Lesson 6 God Gives Elijah Food	The widow feeds Elijah. 1 Kings 17	☒ We can thank God because He gives us food.
Lesson 7 God Shows His Power Through Elijah	Elijah and the prophets of Baal. 1 Kings 18	☒ We can worship God because He is powerful.
Lesson 8 God Brings a Boy Back to Life	The Shunammite's son is raised to life. 2 Kings 4	☒ We can praise God because He can do anything.
Lesson 9 God Heals an Obedient Naaman	God heals Naaman's leprosy. 2 Kings 5	☒ We can obey God's instructions because they are right.

HeartShaper Materials for Unit 2

Early Elementary Activities, **Lessons 5–9 and the Unit 2 Bible Memory Poster and Stickers**

Early Elementary Teaching Pictures, **Lessons 5–9**

Early Elementary Resources

CD

"Show My Love," Tracks 5, 6

"All the Nations You Have Made," Track 7

Bible Memory: *KJV* or *NIV* Additional Bible Memory for Unit 2, *NIV* Bible Memory for Unit 2, *KJV* Bible Memory for Unit 2

Bible Skills Worksheets, Unit 2

Buzzy Bee Letters, Lessons 5–9

Worship Time Ideas, Unit 2

Review Questions, Unit 2

Letter to Families, Unit 2

Posters and Activities: "All the Nations You Have Made" rhythm activity (words), Books of the Old Testament posters, Books of the New Testament posters

Teacher Helps: Attendance Chart, Discipline and Classroom Management, Early Elementary Children, Leading Young Hearts Guide, Safety and Security Issues, Transition Tips

Visuals

Sheet 3 name cards, story figures 7a and 7c; Sheet 4 Bible Memory poster, photo cards, story figures 7b and 7d; Sheet 5 Bible-times headpiece, story figures 8a and 8c, name cards 8b and 8d, story figure 9b; Sheet 6 story figures 9a and 9c

Weekly Bible Reader®, **Issues 5–9**

Faith & Family **online resource,** go to heartshaper.com

Additional Activities for Unit 2

Use these activities for early arrivers, for children who finish activities quickly, and when you are waiting for parents to arrive.

"All the Nations" Bulletin Board

Use the globe from the Unit 1 bulletin board (see page 6). Enlarge the person figure in the narrow column and make enough copies so each child has a few. Create this title in outline letters: "All the nations will worship the Lord." Let the children color the letters and the people figures. Guide the children to mount the people figures on and around the globe .

Alphabet Games

Let the children have fun playing these alphabet games. Have kids sit in a circle. For the first game, have a child start with the letter *A* and tell something about God or something that God has done that begins with that letter. Example: God is **a**wesome. The next child tells something about God that begins with the letter *B*. Example: God has made a **b**eautiful world.

For another alphabet game, have kids name food God gives, using the letters of the alphabet. Example: **a**pple, **b**anana, **c**arrot, and so forth. For an added challenge, the children can also repeat what the kids before them said.

Power Mix

Let the children make a batch of "power mix" to remind them of God's power in providing food for Elijah, the woman, and her son. Provide some or all of the following: raisins, pretzels, O-shaped cereal, small chocolate candies, marshmallows, and small cheese crackers. Have children help mix the food items together and then each can spoon some of the power mix into small resealable bags. They can take home their bags of power mix or enjoy the treat in class.

Fall Wreath

For each child, cut out the center of a paper plate, making the shape of a wreath. Make several leaf patterns on poster board. Tell children to use the leaf patterns to trace and cut out lots of leaves from several fall colors of construction paper. Then children can glue the leaves onto the paper plates. After the wreaths are made, help children punch a hole in each wreath and tie on a yarn hanger. Tell the children that the fall wreaths can remind them of the beautiful fall season given to us by God.

Bible Skills

Make copies of the Bible Skills Worksheets for Unit 2 from the *Resources* CD. For Unit 2, children will understand what a Scripture reference means.

Teaching Tip

For more holiday and seasonal craft ideas, go to heartshaper.com and check out the Teacher Resources under Downloads.

God Cares for Elijah

5

Bible Focus: 1 Kings 16:29–17:6
Bible Memory: All the nations you have made will come and worship before you, Lord; they will bring glory to your name. For you are great and do marvelous deeds; you alone are God (Psalm 86:9, 10).
Life Focus: ⊠ We can praise God because He cares for us.

Heart to Heart

How thankful Elijah must have been that God cared for him by providing him with food and water. God may not send ravens to bring us food, but God does care for us in lots of ways. Can you remember a time when God cared for you in a special way? Maybe God gave you a friend who helped you through a difficult time. Maybe God comforted you during a very sad time in your life. Or maybe God cared for you through the loving actions of your family. As God cares for you in so many ways, remember to thank and praise Him for that care.

Lesson 5 at a Glance

Step			HeartShaper Materials	Other Materials
Step 1 **Focus In** Use one of these activities to help children *discover ways they are cared for.*	≡ *Quick Step* **Caring Ways**	DISCUSS	• none	• none
	Option Caring People	Act It Out	• none	• slips of paper, pen
	Bible Memory *Use this activity to introduce the Bible Memory verses.*	DISCUSS	• none	• Bible
Step 2 **Explore His Word** Use all of these activities to help children *tell how God cared for Elijah* and develop Bible skills.	**God Cares for Elijah**	Bible Story	• *Resources* Sheet 3 name cards, Sheet 5 Bible-times head-piece, CD Track 7 and Review Questions Unit 2 and rhythm activity printable file for Lesson 5; *Teaching Picture* 5	• white board, dry-erase marker, Bibles, clear tape, CD player
	Bible Review Activity	Action		
	Bible Skill Builder and Bible Memory Activity	Bible Skills		
Step 3 **Make It Real** Use one of these activities to help children *explore ways God cares for them.*	≡ *Quick Step* **God Cares for You**	Activity Page	• *Activities* p. 13	• pencils
	Option Drawings of God's Care	Game	• none	• paper, marker, white board, dry-erase markers and erasers
	Option Story from *Weekly Bible Reader*®	LISTEN	• *Weekly Bible Reader*® Issue 5	• none
Step 4 **Live It Out** Use one of these activities to help children *praise God because He cares for them.*	≡ *Quick Step* **God Cares Pennant**	Craft	• reproducible p. 91, *Activities* p. 13	• scissors, glue, markers
	Option Praising God	Music	• *Resources* CD, Sheet 5 Bible-times headpiece	• CD player
	Saying Good-bye		• *Weekly Bible Reader*® Issue 5 and the *Activities* p. 11 Unit 2 Bible Memory poster and stickers	• none

Life Focus
☒ We can praise God because He cares for us.

Step 1 • Use one of these activities to help children **discover ways they are cared for.** Use the Bible Memory activity to introduce the memory verses.

Welcome
- Welcome each child by name.
- Do check-in procedures you follow (name and security tags, offering, attendance chart, etc.).
- Early arrivers will enjoy doing one or more of the activities described on page 32.

≡ *Quick Step* Caring Ways

Let's think about people who care for us and ways they care for us. After I read a sentence, raise your hand and make a "C" with your thumb and forefinger (demonstrate) **if you want to tell us who would care for you in that situation.** Call on several children to respond to each sentence. Tell children that their responses will not all be the same.

1. **I make sure you have food to eat.** 2. **I make sure you have clothes to wear.** 3. **I tell you about God.** 4. **I teach you reading, math, and more.** 5. **I help keep you safe by arresting criminals.** 6. **If you are sick, I help you feel better.** 7. **If you want a hug, you come to me.** 8. **I remember your birthday.** 9. **I help you when you are sad.** 10. **I love you.**

- **What are some other ways you are cared for?** (have a home to live in, have toys and things to have fun with, have a family)

There are lots of ways you are cared for. We're going to learn ways God cares for us and that ☒ we can praise God because He cares for us.

Materials
none

Option Caring People

Let's think about people who care for us and ways they care for us. Before class, write the following on separate slips of paper: mom fixing dinner for the family, dad shopping with a child for clothes, Sunday school teacher teaching children about Jesus, school teacher teaching children about math, sick child at a doctor's office, grandma and grandpa hugging grandchildren and giving them gifts, friend helping a friend who is sad.

Divide the class into two or three small groups. Give each group a situation to act out. Help the groups with ideas as needed. Encourage everyone in the groups to participate. As each group acts out a situation, ask the rest of the class the following questions:

- **What is being acted out?**
- **Who is being cared for?**
- **Who is doing the caring?**

There are lots of ways you are cared for. We're going to learn ways God cares for us and that ☒ we can praise God because He cares for us.

Materials
slips of paper, pen

Teaching Tip
If you have a small class, let each child choose a situation to act out and choose a friend or two to help act out the situation. If you have a large class, divide into several small groups.

Bible Memory Psalm 86:9, 10

The Bible tells us that God does great things. What are some great things God has done? (Accept children's responses.) **Can you do any of those things?** (no) Read aloud Psalm 86:9, 10. **According to these verses, who is going to worship the Lord?** If needed, read verse 9 again. (all the nations) **Who is great?** If needed, read verse 10 again. (God) **Who does marvelous deeds?** (God) **Who alone is God?** (God) **We worship God who cares for us, and ☒ we can praise God because He cares for us.**

Materials
Bible

Transition to Explore His Word
See the *Resources* CD Transition Tips printable file. As children gather, make sure you have all the materials you need.

Explore His Word (20 minutes)

Step 2 • Use all of these activities to help children **tell how God cared for Elijah** and develop Bible skills.

Bible Background for the Teacher

Ahab, son and successor of King Omni of Israel (the northern kingdom), married Jezebel, daughter of the Sidonian king. The marriage was done to officially seal the deal of a political alliance between Israel and Phoenicia.

After Ahab assumed his father's throne, he obtained the distinction of being more wicked than any king who had preceded him. Because of the negative influence of Queen Jezebel and her native religion of Baal, Ahab built an altar and temple to Baal in Israel's capital city of Samaria. Ahab ruthlessly sought to extinguish the worship of Yahweh and make Baal worship the national religion. Likewise, Jezebel was killing off the Lord's prophets (1 Kings 18:4).

God sent the prophet Elijah to Ahab to confront him for his apostasy and to announce God's judgment of drought. Since Baal was a supposed god of rain and storms, the cessation of rain was a direct attack on Israel's idolatry. While God's faithful prophet was hiding from Ahab and being cared for by God, apostate Israel was suffering famine as a result of God's punishment and their new god's inability to care for the country's needs.

Worship Time

If you want to offer a time of worship, see the *Resources* CD Worship Time Ideas printable file for suggestions.

Materials

white board; dry-erase marker; Bibles; *Resources* Sheet 3 name cards, Sheet 5 Bible-times headpiece; clear tape; *Teaching Picture* 5

Before Class

Prepare the Bible-times headpiece. Tape the two headband pieces to the sides of the front piece. Adjust to fit and tape together. Then tape the two other pieces (with wavy bottoms) to the sides of the headpiece.

God Cares for Elijah (1 Kings 16:29–17:6)

Our Bible story comes from the Old Testament book of 1 Kings. Write "1 Kings 16:29" on the board. Point to the Scripture reference as you talk about it. **First Kings is the name of the book, 16 is the chapter number, and 29 is the verse number.** Help children turn to 1 Kings 16:29. Ask for a volunteer to read the verse.

Help me tell today's Bible story. When I say "Elijah" and hold up the Elijah name card (hold it up now), **you need to say "God's prophet." When I say "Ahab" and hold up the Ahab name card** (hold it up now), **you need to say "bad king."** Choose a child to pretend to be Elijah and wear the Bible-times headpiece. This child can also do a little acting during the story. **Listen for how God cared for a man named Elijah.**

Elijah *(hold up name card; kids say "God's prophet")* was a man who worshiped God and wanted to please Him. He was a prophet of God. He told God's important messages to the people.

In the same land where **Elijah** lived was a bad king named **Ahab** *(hold up name card; kids say "bad king")*. He was not a good king. He worshiped idols instead of God. **Ahab** tried to get the people to worship idols instead of worshiping God. **Ahab** did many things that were wrong.

But God had an important message for **Elijah** to give to **King Ahab. Elijah** walked right up to **Ahab** and said, "Ahab! I have a message for you from God. *(Have the child wearing the headpiece shake a finger and look upset.)* You are not a good king. You worship idols. You do not help your people worship the true God either. To punish you for your wickedness, there will be no rain for the next few years."

Can you imagine it not raining for years? The plants used for food would not grow. The ground would become dry and crack. The grass would become brown and die. Animals and people would die because there would be no water to drink. Without plants and animals, people would become very hungry and die.

Well, with a message like that, **King Ahab** probably became very angry with **Elijah.** But God cared for **Elijah.** He told **Elijah** to go and hide near the

Kerith Ravine. *(Have the child wearing the headpiece go to another area of the room.)* God showed **Elijah** where there was a little brook so he could get water. God sent black birds called ravens to bring **Elijah** food. *(Show* Teaching Picture *5.)* The birds brought him bread and meat every morning and evening. God cared for **Elijah.**

Bible Review Activity

How did God care for Elijah? (He had ravens bring Elijah food. God showed Elijah where a brook was so he could get water.) **Let's see what else you remember from the story.** Have the children gather in a circle. Tell the children that they will take turns either holding or wearing the Bible-times headpiece while answering questions about the Bible story. For more questions, see the Review Questions on the *Resources* CD.
- **Who was a prophet of God?** (Elijah)
- **Who was a bad king?** (Ahab)
- **Why was Ahab a bad king?** (He worshiped idols.)
- **What message did Elijah give to King Ahab?** (There would be no rain for a few years.)
- **What would happen without rain for a few years?** (There would be no food. Plants, animals, and people would die.)
- **What did the ravens bring Elijah to eat?** (bread and meat)

God cared for Elijah and God cares for us too. ⊠ **We can praise God because He cares for us.**

Bible Skill Builder and Bible Memory Activity

Write "Psalm 86:9, 10" on the board. Point to the Scripture reference as you talk about it. **Psalms is the name of a book of the Bible. Psalms is in the Old Testament section of the Bible, 86 is the chapter number, and 9 and 10 are the verse numbers.** Have children look in the table of contents in the front of their Bibles. Help them find the Old Testament section and tell them to run their fingers down the list until they see the book of Psalms. Help children find Psalm 86:9, 10 and ask for volunteers to read the verses.

Print and make copies of the words to the "All the Nations You Have Made" rhythm activity. Play "All the Nations You Have Made" from the CD and have kids follow along with the words. Play it again and invite the kids to join in. For added fun, let kids shake bells, shakers, or tambourines while doing the rhythm activity.

All the nations will worship the Lord because He is great. We want to worship and praise God too. ⊠ **We can praise God because He cares for us.**

Materials
Resources Sheet 5
Bible-times headpiece,
CD Review Questions
Unit 2 for Lesson 5 printable file

Materials
white board, dry-erase marker, Bibles, *Resources* CD Track 7 and "All the Nations You Have Made" printable file, CD player (optional: bells, shakers, or tambourines)

Teaching Tip
Print and use the Unit 2 Bible Skills Worksheets found on the *Resources* CD to help children understand what a Scripture reference means.

Make It Real (15 minutes)

Step 3 • Use one of these activities to help children **explore ways God cares for them.**

Materials
Activities p. 13,
pencils

Note
This activity page will also be used in
Step 4.

Materials
paper, marker, white
board, dry-erase markers
and erasers

Teaching Tip
If you have mostly younger children
in your class, you may want to draw
the pictures and let all the kids
guess what you are drawing.

Materials
Weekly Bible Reader®
Issue 5

☰ *Quick Step*   God Cares for You

We've learned that God cared for Elijah by providing him with food and water. Let's explore ways God cares for us. Distribute the activity pages and pencils. Read the directions aloud. Children may enjoy working in pairs on this activity. When all the children are done, hold up one of the activity pages. Point to each picture and ask kids to name the different ways God cares for us.

Ask the pairs of children (or each child) to think of one more way God cares for them besides the ways that are pictured on the activity page. Have each pair of kids act out the additional way God cares for them while the rest of the class guesses what it is.

• **Are there other ways God cares for us?** (He loves us. He gave us Jesus. He gave us the Bible.)

It's great that God cares for us in so many ways. ⊠ We can praise God because He cares for us.

Option   Drawings of God's Care

We've learned that God cared for Elijah by providing him with food and water. Let's explore ways God cares for us as we play a fun guessing game. Before class, write these words on separate slips of paper: clothes, food, water, home, Jesus, Bible, father, mother, grandparents, love, doctor, teachers.

Have a child choose a slip of paper and draw a picture of that person or item on the board. As the child draws, the other children can call out guesses of what is being drawn. Whoever guesses correctly may choose the next slip of paper. After each picture, discuss God's care. Be sure that all children have the opportunity to participate.

• **Are there other ways God cares for us?** (God gives us police officers and firefighters, friends, and a church family to worship with.)

God cares for us in lots of ways. ⊠ We can praise God because He cares for us.

Option   Story from *Weekly Bible Reader®*

We've learned that God cared for Elijah by providing him with food and water. Let's explore ways God cares for us. Read "Change of Seasons."

• **What are some ways God cares for us?** (He loves us. He gave us Jesus. He gave us the Bible. God gives us police officers and firefighters, friends, and a church family to worship with.)

God cares for us in lots of ways. ⊠ We can praise God because He cares for us.

Step 4 • Use one of these activities to help children **praise God because He cares for them.**

Quick Step   God Cares Pennant

We've learned that there are lots of ways God cares for us. ⊠ **We can praise God because He cares for us.** Before class, make copies of the reproducible page. If you did not have the children do the activity page in the *Quick Step* activity in Step 3, let them do it now. After children have completed the puzzle on page 13, have them cut out the pictures. Give children copies of the reproducible page and have them cut out the pennants. They can glue the pictures onto the pennants and then color and decorate the pennants as desired. As they work, continue to talk about God's care.

When all the children are done, have them bring their pennants to a closing prayer circle. Lead the children in praising God for His care. Point to the picture of food. **Repeat after me—I praise You, God, for food.** (Pause so children can repeat each sentence.) Point to the picture of a home. **Repeat after me—I praise You, God, for my home.** Point to the picture of water. **Repeat after me—I praise You, God, for water.** Point to the picture of clothes. **Repeat after me—I praise You, God, for clothes.** Point to the heart. **Repeat after me—I praise You, God, for Your love.** Close with prayer, praising God for His care.

Materials
reproducible p. 91, *Activities* p. 13, scissors, glue, markers

Craft

Added Fun!
Give children paper towel tubes or paint-stirring sticks to attach to their pennants.

Teaching Tip
Copying the pennant onto card stock will make the pennant more durable.

Option   Praising God

We've learned that there are lots of ways God cares for us. ⊠ **We can praise God because He cares for us.** Play "Show My Love" and invite kids to join in singing to praise God. Ask the children to sit or stand in a circle. Tell the children that they will pass the Bible-times headpiece around the circle. When they get the headpiece, they can either put on the headpiece or hold it. Then they are to praise God by saying something that praises Him such as, "God, You are awesome," or "I praise You, God," or something similar. Tell the kids that they can either say the praise to God by themselves, ask a friend to say the praise with them, or ask everyone to say the praise with them. Encourage each child to participate.

Close with prayer. **Dear God, You are great and do marvelous deeds. You alone are God. We praise You. In Jesus' name, amen.**

Materials
Resources CD Tracks 5 and 6, Sheet 5 Bible-times headpiece; CD player

Music

Saying Good-bye

• Distribute Issue 5 of *Weekly Bible Reader*® and the *Activities* page 11 Unit 2 Bible Memory poster and stickers. Stickers are in the middle of *Early Elementary Activities*. Encourage kids to complete their posters at home.

• Make sure children have projects and activity sheets they have done.

• If you have time before parents arrive, use some of the activities on page 32.

• Be sure parents know about the *Faith & Family* page available online to download and use at home. You may want to print and have a copy on display for parents to see. Go to heartshaper.com.

Evaluate
• How eager were the children to praise God for His care?

• How well did the activities you chose help the children learn about God's care?

God Gives Elijah Food

Bible Focus: 1 Kings 17:7-16
Bible Memory: All the nations you have made will come and worship before you, Lord; they will bring glory to your name. For you are great and do marvelous deeds; you alone are God (Psalm 86:9, 10).
Life Focus: ⊠ We can thank God because He gives us food.

Heart to Heart

Apples, oranges, broccoli, nuts, corn, carrots, potatoes, blueberries, strawberries—are you getting hungry? The wide variety of food God has made for us is astonishing! Did you know that there are over 200 categorized types of vegetables? God is great! He could have given us one color of fruit with one type of taste. But God always gives even more than we need—think of the tart lemon and the sweet strawberry.

Food. It's a necessity; we need it to survive. But don't take it for granted. When you enjoy your next meal or midday snack, remember to thank God for your food.

Lesson 6 at a Glance

			HeartShaper Materials	Other Materials
Step 1 **Focus In** Use one of these activities to help children *discuss the need for food.*	*Quick Step* **Favorite Foods**	Game	• reproducible p. 92	• markers
	Option Snack Time	Food	• none	• snack item, napkins
	Bible Memory *Use this activity to introduce the Bible Memory verses.*	Discuss	• none	• world map or globe, Bible
Step 2 **Explore His Word** Use all of these activities to help children *describe how God gave Elijah food* and develop Bible skills.	**God Gives Elijah Food**	Bible Story	• *Resources* Sheet 5 Bible-times headpiece, Sheet 4 Bible Memory poster, CD Review Questions Unit 2 printable file; *Teaching Picture* 6	• white board, dry-erase marker, Bibles, 2 slices or loaves of flat bread, slice of bread, plastic wrap, reusable adhesive
	Bible Review Activity	Game		
	Bible Skill Builder and Bible Memory Activity	Bible Skills		
Step 3 **Make It Real** Use one of these activities to help children *discover ways God gives them food.*	*Quick Step* **God Gives Us Food**	Activity Page	• *Activities* p. 15	• pencils
	Option Food Jump-Up	Action	• none	• grocery ads, scissors
	Option Story from *Weekly Bible Reader®*	Listen	• *Weekly Bible Reader®* Issue 6	• none
Step 4 **Live It Out** Use one of these activities to help children *thank God because He gives them food.*	*Quick Step* **Thank-You Game**	Game	• none	• beanbag
	Option Food Posters	Art	• *Activities* p. 15 and stickers for Lesson 6	• scissors, construction paper, markers, white board, dry-erase marker, glue sticks
	Saying Good-bye		• *Weekly Bible Reader®* Issue 6	• none

Life Focus

☒ We can thank God because He gives us food.

Step 1 • Use one of these activities to help children **discuss the need for food.** Use the Bible Memory activity to introduce the memory verses.

Welcome

- Welcome each child by name.
- Do check-in procedures you follow (name and security tags, offering, attendance chart, etc.).
- Early arrivers will enjoy doing one or more of the activities described on page 32.

═══ *Quick Step*   Favorite Foods

Let's think about why we need food. Before class, make copies of the reproducible page. Distribute the reproducible pages and markers. Read the directions aloud and let children do the page on their own. When everyone is done, let children share what their favorite foods are.

Have children gather in a circle to play a game. Ask a child to name a favorite food beginning with the letter *A.* The next child should name a favorite food beginning with the letter *B.* Continue around the circle, having children use the letters of the alphabet to name favorite foods.

- **Why do we need to eat food?** (gives us energy, helps us grow, to live)
- **What happens if you don't eat for a long time?** (get hungry, feel weak, could eventually die)

God made us so we need food in order to live. And God gives us the food we need. We're going to learn that ☒ we can thank God because He gives us food.

Materials

reproducible p. 92, markers

Option   Snack Time

Let's think about why we need food as we eat a snack. Put a napkin on the table and put one pretzel on the napkin (or whatever snack you are using). **Wow! That looks like a good snack! Everybody can enjoy the pretzel!** The children should be complaining that one pretzel isn't enough. Add one or two more pretzels. **That's enough, isn't it?** Keep adding a few pretzels at a time and asking the kids if that is enough. Eventually put out enough pretzels for all to enjoy. As kids enjoy the snack, ask:

- **Why do we need to eat food?** (gives us energy, helps us grow, to live)
- **What happens if you don't eat for a long time?** (get hungry, feel weak, could eventually die)

God made us so we need food in order to live. And God gives us the food we need. We're going to learn that ☒ we can thank God because He gives us food.

Materials

snack item (pretzels, raisins, or crackers), napkins

Bible Memory   Psalm 86:9, 10

Show the children a world map or a globe. Read aloud Psalm 86:9. **Our Bible Memory verses say that all the nations will worship the Lord. Who would like to point to a nation or country on the map?** As a child points to a location, have the children name the country or you name it. Let several children point to locations on the map. Read aloud Psalm 86:9, 10. **Who will worship the Lord?** (all the nations) **Only God is great and does marvelous deeds. One great thing God does is that He gives us food. We're going to learn that ☒ we can thank God because He gives us food.**

Materials

world map or globe, Bible

Transition to Explore His Word

See the *Resources* CD Transition Tips printable file. As children gather, make sure you have all the materials you need.

Explore His Word (20 minutes)

Step 2 • Use all of these activities to help children **describe how God gave Elijah food** and develop Bible skills.

Bible Background for the Teacher

The brook providing Elijah with water eventually dried up. The divinely instituted drought and subsequent famine persisted due to Israel's making Baal worship her national religion. Instead of continuing to feed Elijah bread and meat brought by ravens, God told Elijah to go and find a certain widow in Zarephath of Sidon, or Phoenicia. Ironically, Phoenicia is Queen Jezebel's homeland, the place from where she imported the religion of Baal to Israel.

When Elijah meets up with the impoverished widow, she is gathering her supplies to make one last meal for herself and her son. Unlike Israel, the widow of Zarephath (a non-Israelite), at the request of God's spokesman, Elijah, acted in faith and gave all that she had. And in return she miraculously received an unending supply of food for herself, her son, and Elijah. What a contrast to the nation of Israel (identified as God's chosen people) who forfeited God's promises and suffered the consequences of drought and famine because of their disobedience and treason.

Worship Time

If you want to offer a time of worship, see the *Resources* CD Worship Time Ideas printable file for suggestions.

Materials

white board, dry-erase marker, Bibles, *Resources* Sheet 5 Bible-times headpiece used in Lesson 5, 2 loaves of flat bread (or 2 slices of regular bread), *Teaching Picture 6*

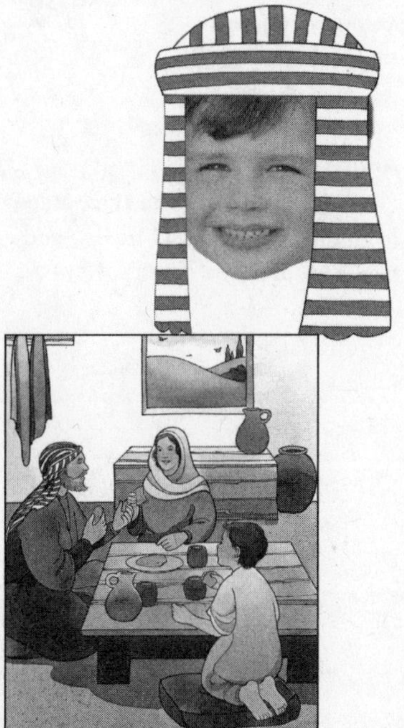

God Gives Elijah Food   (1 Kings 17:7-16)

Our Bible story comes from the book of 1 Kings. Write "1 Kings 17:7" on the board. **Is 1 Kings in the Old Testament or New Testament?** (Old) Point to the Scripture reference as you talk about it. **First Kings is the name of the book. What is the chapter number?** (17) **Seven is the verse number.** Help children turn to 1 Kings 17:7. Ask for a volunteer to read the verse.

Choose a child to wear the Bible-times headpiece and portray Elijah during the story. Choose another child to portray the woman. Guide them to act out the story as you tell it. **Everyone needs to listen for how God gave Elijah food.**

There had been no water for a long time. Elijah had delivered his message to wicked King Ahab, and God had kept His word. There had been no rain for so long that the brooks dried up. Food and water were hard to find for both people and animals. But God had taken care of Elijah at the Kerith Ravine. Do you remember how God took care of Elijah? (God had provided a brook for Elijah to drink water from and had sent ravens to bring him bread and meat.)

Then God told Elijah to go to a city called Zarephath (Zair-uh-fath) to meet a woman. *(Have Elijah walk to a different part of the room.)* God had commanded a woman to help take care of Elijah.

When Elijah came to the gate of the city, he saw a woman gathering sticks to make a fire. *(Have the woman bend over and pretend to be gathering sticks.)* Elijah asked her, "Would you please bring me some water? I am thirsty." *(Elijah can motion to the woman.)* Elijah also asked her for a piece of bread.

The woman answered, "I have no bread. I have only a little flour and oil. These sticks I am gathering are for a fire. I will take them home and cook a meal over the fire for my son and me. It will be our last meal."

But Elijah had some wonderful news for this woman and her son. He told her, "You don't have to be afraid or worry. Go home and cook your food. But first make for me a small loaf of bread from the flour and oil you have and bring it to me. Then cook something for yourself and your son. God says that your jar of flour will never become empty, and your jug of oil will always have oil in it, until God gives rain again."

So the woman went back to her home and did exactly what Elijah told her to do. *(Have the woman walk to a different part of the room.)* She first made

Explore His Word (continued)

a loaf of bread for Elijah. *(Give the woman a slice or loaf of bread to give to Elijah.)* Then she was able to make a loaf of bread for herself and her son because there was plenty of flour and oil left. *(Give the woman a slice or loaf of bread to hold.)* God gave Elijah, the woman, and her son the food they needed. *(Show Teaching Picture 6.)*

Bible Review Activity

How did God give Elijah food? (God worked through the woman in Zarephath to give Elijah food. God caused the woman's jar of flour and jug of oil to never run out so she could always make bread.) **Let's see what else you remember from the story.** Have the children gather in a circle. Put a slice of bread in plastic wrap. Tell the children to pass the bread around the circle until you say "flour and oil." Whoever is holding the bread can answer a question. Make sure that everyone gets to answer at least one question. For more questions, see the Review Questions on the CD.

• **Why did God tell Elijah to go to Zarephath?** (to meet a woman who could take care of him)

• **What did Elijah ask the woman for?** (water and bread)

• **Why was the woman gathering sticks?** (to make a fire to cook a last meal for herself and her son)

• **What did Elijah tell the woman to do?** (first make him some bread and then make something for herself and her son)

• **What did God cause to happen to the woman's jar of flour and jug of oil?** (They never ran out.)

God gave Elijah, the woman, and her son the food they needed. I'm sure they thanked God for the food He gave them. ⊠ We can thank God because He gives us food too!

Bible Skill Builder and Bible Memory Activity

Write "Psalm 86:9, 10" on the board. **When we want to look up something in our Bibles we have to know several things. We have to know the name of the book.** Ask a child to come to the board and point to the name of the book. (Psalm) **We have to know the chapter number.** Ask a child to point to the chapter number. (86) **We have to know the verse numbers.** Ask a child to point to the verse numbers. (9 and 10) Help the children find Psalm 86:9, 10 in their Bibles and ask for volunteers to read the verses.

Display the Bible Memory poster. **This poster has our Bible Memory verses on it.** Point to the words and pictures as you read the verses. Invite the children to read it with you while you point to the words and pictures. **All the nations will worship the Lord because He is great. We want to worship and thank God too. ⊠ We can thank God because He gives us food.**

Materials
slice of bread, plastic wrap, *Resources* CD Review Questions Unit 2 for Lesson 6 printable file

Added Fun!
Let the children enjoy some bread with jelly or margarine.

Materials
white board, dry-erase marker, Bibles, *Resources* Sheet 4 Bible Memory poster, reusable adhesive

Added Fun!
Play "All the Nations You Have Made" from the *Resources* CD Track 7 and have kids join in.

Make It Real (15 minutes)

Step 3 • Use one of these activities to help children **discover ways God gives them food.**

Materials
Activities p. 15,
pencils

Note
This activity page will also be used in
Step 4.

☰ *Quick Step* God Gives Us Food

We've learned that God gave Elijah food by giving the woman in Zarephath enough flour and oil so she could always make bread. Let's discover ways God gives us food. Distribute the activity pages and pencils. Read the directions aloud and do the page together. Ask for a volunteer to tell where the loaf of bread comes from. (wheat) Ask for a volunteer to tell where the egg comes from. (chicken) Do the same with all the photos in Column B. As time permits, have children name other foods while the rest of the class guesses where those foods come from.

• **What are some other ways God gives us food?** (God gives soil to plant crops. God gives rain and sun to help food grow. God gives us parents and families to buy food.)

There are lots of ways God gives us food. ⊠ **We can thank God because He gives us food.**

Materials
grocery advertisements,
scissors

Option Food Jump-Up

We've learned that God gave Elijah food by giving the woman in Zarephath enough flour and oil so she could always make bread. Let's discover ways God gives us food. Distribute the grocery ads and scissors. Ask kids to find two or three pictures of food and cut them out. Have the children show their food pictures. Ask the children to identify each food and ask:

• **How does God gives us that kind of food?** (Help the children as needed to think through how God provides that kind of food.)

Then lead the kids in playing a game with the food pictures.

Jump up if God sends rain so one of your food items can grow.

Jump up if God uses soil so one of your food items can grow.

Jump up if God uses cornstalks or wheat shocks so we can eat one of your food items.

Jump up if God uses parents and families to buy one of your food items.

Jump up if God gives sunlight so one of your food items can grow.

Jump up if God uses cows to give us one of your food items.

Jump up if God uses chickens to give us one of your food items.

There are lots of ways God gives us food. ⊠ **We can thank God because He gives us food.**

Materials
Weekly Bible Reader® Issue 6

Option Story from *Weekly Bible Reader*®

We've learned that God gave Elijah food by giving the woman in Zarephath enough flour and oil so she could always make bread. Let's discover ways God gives us food. Read "Burgers and Fries."

• **What are some ways God gives us food?** (God gives soil, seeds, rain, and sun. God gives us parents and families to buy food. God gives us cows and chickens.)

There are lots of ways God gives us food. ⊠ **We can thank God because He gives us food.**

Step 4 • Use one of these activities to help children **thank God because He gives them food.**

≡ *Quick Step*   Thank-You Game

We've learned that there are lots of ways God gives us food. We're going to play a game to help us remember ⊠ we can thank God because He gives us food. Have the children sit or stand in a circle. Tell the children that you will toss the beanbag to one of them and that child should say "Thank You, God, for ___," naming a favorite food. That child should toss the beanbag back to you and you toss it to another child. Continue until everyone has had at least one turn to thank God for food.

Close with a time of prayer. Invite children to thank God for all the food He gives us.

Materials
beanbag

Game

Option   Food Posters

We've learned that there are lots of ways God gives us food. We're going to make food posters to remember ⊠ we can thank God because He gives us food. If you did not have children do the *Activities* page 15 in Step 3, let them do it now. Then tell the kids to cut out the food items in Column B. Give each child a sheet of construction paper, the food stickers, and markers. Write on the board "Thank You, God!" and encourage the children to write this at the top of the construction paper. Tell the children to make food posters by gluing on the food photos and pressing on the food stickers in any way they desire. They can draw food items on their posters too.

Have kids bring their food posters to a closing prayer circle. Let the children show their food posters. Ask the children to pray and thank God for one or two food items on their posters.

Materials
Activities p. 15 and stickers for Lesson 6, scissors, construction paper, markers, white board, dry-erase marker, glue sticks

Art

Saying Good-bye
• Distribute Issue 6 of *Weekly Bible Reader.*®
• Make sure children have projects and activity sheets they have done.
• If you have time before parents arrive, use some of the activities on page 32.
• Remind parents that a weekly *Faith & Family* page is available online to print and use with their child at home. Go to heartshaper.com.

Evaluate
• How did the children demonstrate they understood that God gives us food?
• Did you give all children the opportunity to ask and answer questions?

God Shows His Power Through Elijah 7

Bible Focus: 1 Kings 18:18-39

Bible Memory: All the nations you have made will come and worship before you, Lord; they will bring glory to your name. For you are great and do marvelous deeds; you alone are God (Psalm 86:9, 10).

Life Focus: ⊠ We can worship God because He is powerful.

Heart to Heart

God asked Elijah to do a hard thing. He was one man up against hundreds and everyone was watching. Do you ever feel that way? Are you the only one at your workplace that doesn't lie about the hours worked? Are you the only one that speaks up for what is right at a school board meeting? If so, remember how God showed His power through Elijah. God can also show His power through you. Remember that we serve a powerful God!

Lesson 7 at a Glance

		HeartShaper Materials	Other Materials
Step 1 **Focus In** Use one of these activities to help children *explore powerful things.*	⹀ *Quick Step* **Powerful Things** (Game)	• *Resources* Sheet 4 photo cards	• white board, dry-erase markers and erasers
	Option Mixing Power (Object Lesson)	• none	• flour, measuring cup, large bowl, water, container, fork, wisk, electric mixer
	Bible Memory *Use this activity to introduce the Bible Memory verses.* (DISCUSS)	• none	• Bible
Step 2 **Explore His Word** Use all of these activities to help children *tell how God showed His power through Elijah* and develop Bible skills.	**God Shows His Power Through Elijah** (Bible Story)	• *Resources* Sheet 3 name cards, Sheets 3 and 4 story figures 7a–7d, Sheet 5 Bible-times headpiece, CD; *Teaching Picture* 7; *Activities* p. 17	• white board, dry-erase marker, Bibles, poster board, reusable adhesive, pencils or markers, CD player
	Bible Review Activity (Activity Page)		
	Bible Skill Builder and Bible Memory Activity (Bible Skills)		
Step 3 **Make It Real** Use one of these activities to help children *list ways to worship God because He is powerful.*	⹀ *Quick Step* **I Can Worship!** (Activity Page)	• *Activities* p. 18 and corresponding stickers	• pencils or markers
	Option Ways to Worship Cube (Action)	• reproducible p. 93	• scissors, clear tape
	Option Story from *Weekly Bible Reader®* (LISTEN)	• *Weekly Bible Reader®* Issue 7	• none
Step 4 **Live It Out** Use one of these activities to help children *worship God because He is powerful.*	⹀ *Quick Step* **Worship Posters** (Sing & Pray)	• *Activities* p. 18, *Resources* CD	• scissors, construction paper, markers, glue, white board, dry-erase marker, CD player
	Option Worship Cubes (Pray)	• cubes made in Step 3	• none
	Saying Good-bye	• *Weekly Bible Reader®* Issue 7	• none

Focus In (15 minutes)

Step 1 • Use one of these activities to help children **explore powerful things.** Use the Bible Memory activity to introduce the memory verses.

Welcome
- Welcome each child by name.
- Do check-in procedures you follow (name and security tags, offering, attendance chart, etc.).
- Early arrivers will enjoy doing one or more of the activities described on page 32.

≡ *Quick Step* Powerful Things

Let's think about powerful things. Tell the children that you have photo cards of some powerful things. Ask for a volunteer to choose a photo. The child should either draw that powerful thing on the board or act out that powerful thing while everyone guesses what it is. Do the same with all the photo cards. Ask the following about each photo:
- **Why is a _____ a powerful thing?**
- **What are some other powerful things?** (tornado, elephants, whales)

There are lots of powerful things. We're going to learn that God is powerful and that ⊠ we can worship God because He is powerful.

Materials
Resources Sheet 4 photo cards, white board, dry-erase markers and erasers

Added Fun!
Let children draw pictures or act out other powerful things not pictured on the photo cards.

Option   Mixing Power

Let's think about powerful things. Before class, put one or two cups of flour in a large bowl and one half cup of water in a container. **I need you to help me mix this flour and water together.** Pour a little of the water into the flour and have a volunteer stir the mix with a fork. **I think we need something with more power.** Pour a little more water into the mix and have another volunteer stir the mix with a whisk. **This whisk is bigger and has more power. What could we use that has even more power?** (electric mixer) Pour the rest of the water into the mix and let a volunteer use the electric mixer.
- **Which one of the mixing tools had the most power?** (electric mixer)
- **When you think of powerful things, what do you think of?** (tornado, hurricane, lion, elephant, lightning, tsunami, fire, volcano)

There are lots of powerful things. We're going to learn that God is powerful and that ⊠ we can worship God because He is powerful.

Materials
flour, measuring cup, large bowl, water, container, fork, whisk, electric mixer

Bible Memory   Psalm 86:9, 10

Read aloud Psalm 86:9, 10. **According to these Bible verses, what has God made?** (all the nations) **Be thinking of other things God has made.** Divide the class into two groups. Tell each group that they will each have five seconds to name something God has made. If a group doesn't name something in five seconds, the other group can take its turn. Continue as time permits. **God is powerful and made everything! We're going to learn that ⊠ we can worship God because He is powerful.**

Materials
Bible

Transition to Explore His Word
See the *Resources* CD Transition Tips printable file. As children gather, make sure you have all the materials you need.

⊠ We can worship God because He is powerful.

Explore His Word (20 minutes)

Step 2 • Use all of these activities to help children **tell how God showed His power through Elijah** and develop Bible skills.

Bible Background for the Teacher

It had been over three years since Elijah announced God's message of drought upon Israel for abandoning God and replacing Him with the worship of the false god, Baal. Elijah had been in seclusion all this time, although King Ahab had been searching for him. Elijah reappeared and challenged Ahab to a public contest for all to see the power and identification of the one true God. All day long Baal's prophets called out to him with no response. They even cut themselves with knives in a desperate attempt to arouse Baal to action. Baal, the god of storms, had been unable to send rain to end the drought and was now just as powerless to send fire to light his own altar.

Elijah rebuilt the abandoned altar of the Lord with 12 stones representing the 12 tribes of Israel. He then prayed to the God of Abraham, Isaac, and Israel—reminding Israel of its spiritual heritage and covenant relationship to Yahweh. Elijah even drenched the altar and the sacrifice with jars of water to show everyone that he was not using any tricks. Baal was proven to be a fraud.

Worship Time

If you want to offer a time of worship, see the *Resources* CD Worship Time Ideas printable file for suggestions.

Materials

white board; dry-erase marker; Bibles; *Resources* Sheet 3 name cards, Sheets 3 and 4 story figures 7a–7d, Sheet 5 Bible-times headpiece used in previous lessons; poster board; reusable adhesive; *Teaching Picture* 7

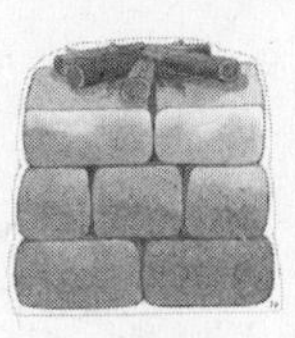
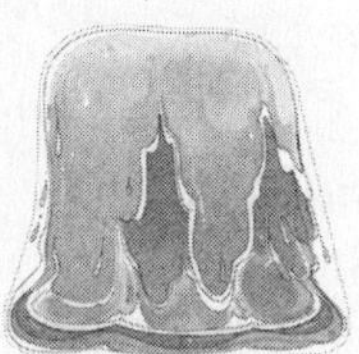

God Shows His Power Through Elijah (1 Kings 18:18-39)

Our Bible story once again comes from the book of 1 Kings. Write "1 Kings 18:19" on the board. **Is 1 Kings in the Old Testament or New Testament?** (Old) Point to the Scripture reference as you talk about it. **The name of the book is ___** (invite children to respond together). **The chapter number is ___. The verse number is ___.** Help children turn to 1 Kings 18:19. Ask for a volunteer to read the first part of the verse.

Help me tell today's Bible story. When I say "Elijah" and hold up the Elijah name card (hold it up now), **you need to say "God's prophet." When I say "Ahab" and hold up the Ahab name card** (hold it up now), **you need to say "bad king."** Choose a child to portray Elijah, wearing the Bible-times headpiece and doing a little acting during the story. **Everyone needs to listen for how God showed His power through Elijah.**

Elijah *(hold up name card; kids say "God's prophet")* was a prophet of God. He told people about God. **Elijah** loved God, and he wanted **King Ahab** *(hold up name card; kids say "bad king")* and the people to know once and for all how great and powerful God is. So **Elijah** asked **King Ahab** and the people to come together for a contest.

"Let's have a contest between your god, Baal (Bay-ul), and the true living God," said **Elijah.** "If Baal is god, do what he says. But if the Lord is God, then follow and obey Him!" *(Have the child portraying Elijah point upward.)*

King Ahab, the people, and the 450 prophets of Baal gathered together. **Elijah** suggested that the 450 prophets offer an animal sacrifice on an altar to their god, Baal. And **Elijah** would offer an animal sacrifice to God. The god who would send fire to burn up the animal sacrifice would be the true God. The 450 prophets of Baal went first.

(Attach 7a to the poster board with reusable adhesive.) The 450 prophets of Baal made their altar out of stone and put an animal sacrifice on it. They prayed and cried out to Baal. But nothing happened to the animal sacrifice on the altar. They cried even louder and harder. They shouted, "Baal, please answer us!" But still there was no answer. *(Remove 7a.)*

Then **Elijah** built his altar to God. *(Show 7a.)* He used 12 stones to build the altar. *(Have the child portraying Elijah pretend to build.)* He put the animal sacrifice on the altar. **Elijah** dug a ditch around the altar he made. "Bring water and pour it on everything," he commanded. Water was poured on the animal sacrifice, the stones, and the wood. *(Put 7b over the altar.)* "Bring more water," **Elijah** said two more times. By now, the sacrifice and the altar were soaking wet. *(Show* Teaching Picture 7.*)* Then **Elijah** looked to Heaven and prayed, "God, let these people know that You are the true God." *(Have the child portraying Elijah look upward and fold his hands.)*

(Put 7c on top of the altar and 7d at the base of the altar.) God sent down a fire so powerful that it not only burned up the animal sacrifice, the fire also burned up the wood, the water, and even the stones themselves. The entire altar was gone! *(Remove all the figures.)* Usually water and stones don't burn, but God is so powerful He could do even that!

All the people fell down and cried out over and over, "The Lord—he is God! The Lord—he is God!"

Bible Review Activity

How did God show His power through Elijah? (God sent a fire that burned up the sacrifice that Elijah made to Him. The fire was so powerful that it also burned up the stone altar and the water.) **Let's see what else you remember from the story.** Distribute the activity pages and pencils or markers. Read the directions aloud and do the page together. Then do the following fun activity with the children.

If Elijah was a prophet of God, say "God's prophet." (God's prophet)

If King Ahab and the people worshiped a sports star, jump up and down. (no)

If the prophets of Baal shouted and cried to Baal, shout "Baal, hear us!" (shout)

If Elijah used 50 stones to build his altar, count to 50. (no)

If Elijah had water poured on his sacrifice and on the altar, say "water, water, water." (water, water, water)

If Elijah prayed to God, fold your hands. (fold hands)

If God sent a powerful fire that burned up the sacrifice, the altar, and the water, say "The Lord—he is God!" (The Lord—he is God!)

God showed His power through Elijah. Just as all the people did when they saw God's power, ⊠ we can worship God because He is powerful.

Materials
Activities p. 17, pencils or markers

Bible Skill Builder and Bible Memory Activity

Write "Psalm 86:9, 10" on the board. Point to the Scripture reference as you talk about it. **Psalms is the name of a book of the Bible. Psalms is in the Old Testament section of the Bible. What is the chapter number?** (86) **What are the verse numbers?** (9 and 10) Have children look in the table of contents in the front of their Bibles. Help them find the Old Testament section and tell them to run their fingers down the list until they see the book of Psalms. Help children find Psalm 86: 9, 10 and ask for volunteers to read the verses.

Distribute copies of the words to the "All the Nations You Have Made" rhythm activity. Play "All the Nations You Have Made" from the CD and invite the children to join in. For added fun, let kids shake bells, shakers, or tambourines while doing the rhythm activity.

Elijah and the people saw God's great power and worshiped Him. ⊠ We can worship God because He is powerful.

Materials
white board, dry-erase marker, Bibles, *Resources* CD Track 7, CD player (optional: bells, shakers, or tambourines)

Bible Skills

Teaching Tip
Print and use the Unit 2 Bible Skills Worksheets found on the *Resources* CD to help children understand what a Scripture reference means.

Life Focus

◻ We can worship God because He is powerful.

Materials
Activities p. 18 and corresponding stickers, pencils or markers

Activity Page

Note
Page 18 is also used in Step 4.

Materials
reproducible p. 93, scissors, clear tape

Action

Teaching Tip
Copying the cube onto card stock will make the cube more durable for tossing.

Materials
Weekly Bible Reader® Issue 7

LISTEN

Make It Real (15 minutes)

Step 3 • Use one of these activities to help children **list ways to worship God because He is powerful.**

≡ *Quick Step*   I Can Worship!

We've learned that God showed His power through Elijah. Let's think of ways to worship God because He is powerful. Distribute the activity pages, stickers, and pencils or markers. Read the directions aloud and do the page together. When the children are finished, ask for volunteers to tell how they completed the last sentence.

• **How many of you can worship God by singing a song to God?** (Ask kids to raise their hands.)

• **How many of you can worship God by praying and telling God He is great?**

• **How many of you can worship God by giving money to God?**

• **How many of you can worship God by telling others about God?**

• **What are some other ways to worship God?** (go to a church service, listen to Bible stories, read the Bible)

There are lots of ways to worship God. ◻ We can worship God because He is powerful.

Option   Ways to Worship Cube

We've learned that God showed His power through Elijah. Let's think of ways to worship God because He is powerful. Before class, make copies of the reproducible page and put together one of the cubes. If you have a large class, make several cubes. Ask the children to sit in a circle and take turns tossing the cube. The kids should read whatever is on top of the cube and answer the question. If a child needs help answering a question, let him ask a friend for help. When the cube reads "We worship You, God. You are powerful!" all the kids should stand and say that together. Be sure that everyone has the opportunity to participate. Then give kids copies of the reproducible page and let children make their own cubes.

• **What are some ways to worship God?** (pray, sing, and give money to God; tell others about God; go to a church service; listen to Bible stories; read the Bible)

There are lots of ways to worship God. ◻ We can worship God because He is powerful.

Option   Story from *Weekly Bible Reader*®

We've learned that God showed His power through Elijah. Let's think of ways to worship God because He is powerful. Read "Kimi's Prayer."

• **What are some ways to worship God?** (pray, sing, and give money to God; tell others about God; go to a church service; listen to Bible stories; read the Bible)

There are lots of ways to worship God. ◻ We can worship God because He is powerful.

Step 4 • Use one of these activities to help children **worship God because He is powerful.**

≡ *Quick Step* Worship Posters

⊠ **We can worship God because He is powerful. And we've learned that there are lots of ways to worship God. So let's worship God because He is powerful.** If you did not have the children do *Activities* page 18 in Step 3, have them do it now. Distribute construction paper, markers, scissors, glue, and the activity pages. Write "Worship God" on the board and have kids print this title at the top of their construction paper. Ask kids to cut out the altars and attach them to sheets of construction paper. (Make sure page 18 is facing outward.) Let kids decorate their pages as desired.

We're going to sing and pray to worship God right now. Play "Show My Love" and invite kids to join in singing to worship God.

Then lead the children in a prayer time. Tell the children that you will pray sentence prayers, and they are to respond by praying the following after each sentence, "We worship You, God. You are powerful." **Dear God, You are powerful.** (pause; kids pray) **You cared for Elijah and You care for us.** (pause; kids pray) **You gave Elijah food and You give us food.** (pause; kids pray) **You heard Elijah's prayer and You hear our prayers.** (pause; kids pray) **In Jesus' name, amen.**

Materials

Activities p. 18, scissors, construction paper, markers, glue, whiteboard, dry-erase marker, *Resources* CD Tracks 5 and 6, CD player

Teaching Tip

The altar can also be taped along one side to the construction paper so that both sides can be viewed.

Option   Worship Cubes

⊠ **We can worship God because He is powerful. And we've learned that there are lots of ways to worship God. So let's worship God because He is powerful.** If children did not make the cubes in Step 3, let kids make them now.

Have children bring their cubes to a closing time of prayer. **Your worship cubes will help you remember that you can worship God in lots of ways. Turn your cubes so you can see the words "We worship You, God. You are powerful!"** Tell the children that together they will worship God by saying these words. Divide the class into two groups. Group one will say "We worship You, God." Group two will say "You are powerful!" Tell children to close their eyes as you lead the groups in praying their worship sentence several times. Close by praying quietly, **We worship You, God. You are powerful. In Jesus' name, amen.**

Materials

cubes made in Step 3

Saying Good-bye

• Distribute Issue 7 of *Weekly Bible Reader.*®
• Make sure children have projects and activity sheets they have done.
• If you have time before parents arrive, use some of the activities on page 32.
• Remind parents that a weekly *Faith & Family* page is available online to print and use with their child at home. Go to heartshaper.com.

Evaluate

• How willing were the children to worship God?
• How can you help all the children know that you care about them?

God Brings a Boy Back to Life 

Bible Focus: 2 Kings 4:8-37
Bible Memory: All the nations you have made will come and worship before you, Lord; they will bring glory to your name. For you are great and do marvelous deeds; you alone are God (Psalm 86:9, 10).
Life Focus: ⊠ We can praise God because He can do anything.

Heart to Heart

What an amazing fact that God can do anything! Because we have so many limitations, it is difficult to grasp that God has none of those limitations. When you struggle with negative thoughts, remember that God can do anything. When you don't know where money for next week's food will come from, remember that God can do anything. When you are having health problems, remember that God can do anything. When you have trouble loving all the children in your class, remember that God can do anything. God can do anything—praise Him!

Lesson 8 at a Glance

		HeartShaper Materials	Other Materials
Step 1 **Focus In** Use one of these activities to help children *explore things they can and cannot do.*	*Quick Step* **I Can, I Can't** 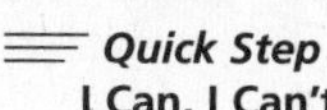	• *Activities* p. 19	• pencils
	Option If You Can 	• none	• none
	Bible Memory *Use this activity to introduce the Bible Memory verses.* 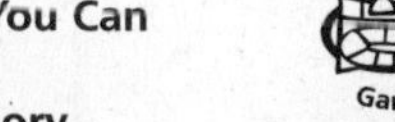	• *Resources* Sheet 4 Bible Memory poster	• Bible
Step 2 **Explore His Word** Use all of these activities to help children *tell how God brought a boy back to life* and develop Bible skills.	**God Brings a Boy Back to Life** 	• *Resources* Sheet 5 story figures 8a, 8c, and name cards 8b, 8d, CD Review Questions Unit 2 printable file, Sheet 4 Bible Memory poster; *Teaching Picture* 8	• white board, dry-erase marker, Bibles, craft sticks, clear tape, reusable adhesive, self-stick notes
	Bible Review Activity 		
	Bible Skill Builder and Bible Memory Activity 		
Step 3 **Make It Real** Use one of these activities to help children *identify times God has shown He can do anything.*	*Quick Step* **God Can Do Anything!** 	• *Activities* p. 20 and corresponding stickers	• colored pencils or markers
	Option It's in the Bag 	• none	• large bag; leaf; water in a clear container; pictures of a person, the ark, and baby Jesus
	Option Story from Weekly Bible Reader® 	• *Weekly Bible Reader®* Issue 8	• none
Step 4 **Live It Out** Use one of these activities to help children *praise God because He can do anything.*	*Quick Step* **I Praise You, God!** 	• none	• none
	Option Praises 	• none	• large bag; leaf; water in a clear container; pictures of a person, the ark, and baby Jesus
	Saying Good-bye	• *Weekly Bible Reader®* Issue 8	• none

Focus In (15 minutes)

Step 1 • Use one of these activities to help children **explore things they can and cannot do.** Use the Bible Memory activity to introduce the memory verses.

Welcome
- Welcome each child by name.
- Do check-in procedures you follow (name and security tags, offering, attendance chart, etc.).
- Early arrivers will enjoy doing one or more of the activities described on page 32.

≡ *Quick Step* I Can, I Can't

Let's think about things we can and can't do. Distribute the activity pages and pencils. Read the directions aloud. Let the children complete the page on their own. When everyone is done, say, **Raise your hand if you can fly like a bird. Raise your hand if you can drive a car. Raise your hand if you can ride a bike.** Do the same for all the pictures.
- **What are some other things you can do?** (accept children's responses)
- **What are some other things you can't do?** (accept children's responses)

There are lots of things we can do and lots of things we can't do. But who can do anything? (God) **We're going to learn that ☒ we can praise God because He can do anything.**

Materials
Activities p. 19, pencils

Activity Page

Added Fun!
Let kids act out things they can and can't do while the rest of the class guesses what they are doing.

Option If You Can

Let's think about things we can and can't do as we play a fun game. Have kids line up across the room from you. Tell the children that if you say something they *can* do, they are to take one medium-size step forward. If you say something they *can't* do, they are to take a baby step backward. Keep going until all the children reach you.

If you can eat ice cream, take a step forward. If you can ride a bike, take a step forward. If you can love Jesus, take a step forward. If you can make a tree, take a step forward. If you can make a rainbow, take a step forward. If you can draw a picture, take a step forward. If you can brush your teeth, take a step forward. If you can drive a car, take a step forward. If you can tie your own shoes, take a step forward.
- **What are some other things you can do?** (accept children's responses)
- **What are some other things you can't do?** (accept children's responses)

There are lots of things we can do and lots of things we can't do. We're going to learn that ☒ we can praise God because He can do anything.

Materials
none

Game

Added Fun!
Play the game again and let a couple kids be the leader and name things kids can and can't do.

Bible Memory Psalm 86:9, 10

Show kids the Bible Memory poster but turn it upside down. **Can we read the Bible Memory verses together?** (Kids should say no.) Turn the poster so kids see the back of the poster. **Now can we say the verses?** Hold the poster behind your back. **Now can we say the verses? There are some things we just can't do.** Read aloud Psalm 86:9, 10. **Who is worthy of worship, is great, and does marvelous deeds?** (God) **Who can do anything?** (God) **We're going to learn that ☒ we can praise God because He can do anything.**

Materials
Resources Sheet 4 Bible Memory poster, Bible

DISCUSS

Transition to Explore His Word
See the *Resources* CD Transition Tips printable file. As children gather, make sure you have all the materials you need.

Explore His Word (20 minutes)

Step 2 • Use all of these activities to help children **tell how God brought a boy back to life** and develop Bible skills.

Bible Background for the Teacher

This account tells about God's power through two miracles. The Shunammite woman somehow recognized that Elisha was doing the work of the Lord. By providing for Elisha, the woman helped Elisha continue his holy work.

At this time in history, not having a son was a huge disappointment for a family. Sons carried on the family name and provided for their widowed mothers. This woman was likely familiar with the history of her people and the account of Abraham and Sarah who were both well beyond the age of childbearing and yet God blessed them with a son (see Genesis 18:10-14; Hebrews 11:11).

The Shunammite's son died suddenly after a vaguely described illness, possibly heat stroke. When the woman went to Elisha, she held onto his feet to add force to her request. The manner of the miracle Elisha performs is very similar to the one performed by his predecessor and mentor, Elijah (1 Kings 17:19-22). In both miracles the prophets prayed and stretched themselves out on the dead boys' bodies and by God's power were then able to return the resurrected boys to their awe-filled mothers.

Worship Time

If you want to offer a time of worship, see the *Resources* CD Worship Time Ideas printable file for suggestions.

Materials

white board; dry-erase marker; Bibles; *Resources* Sheet 5 story figures 8a, 8c, and name cards 8b, 8d; craft sticks; clear tape; *Teaching Picture* 8

Before Class

Attach craft sticks to the backs of the story figures.

Teaching Tip

Show a picture of a Bible-times house with a flat roof. This will help the children understand how a room could be built on a roof.

God Brings a Boy Back to Life   (2 Kings 4:8-37)

Our Bible story comes from the book of 2 Kings. Write "2 Kings 4:8" on the board. **We know that 1 Kings is in the Old Testament. Do you think 2 Kings is in the Old or New Testament?** (Old) Point to the Scripture reference as you talk about it. **Second Kings is the name of the book, 4 is the chapter number, and 8 is the verse number.** Help children turn to 2 Kings 4:8. Ask for a volunteer to read the verse.

Help me tell today's Bible story. When I hold up this name card (hold 8b up now), **you need to say "woman." When I hold up this name card** (hold 8d up now), **you need to say "son." And you need to listen for how God brought a boy back to life.** You may want to give the story figures to children to hold during the story.

(Show 8a.) Elisha was a prophet of God. One day he visited the city of Shunem (Shoo-nem). A *(hold up card 8b; kids say "woman")* invited him to eat a meal with her family. So whenever he went to Shunem, Elisha was invited to stay and share a meal with the *(card 8b)* and her family. This *(card 8b)* encouraged her husband to build a room for Elisha on the roof of the house. The *(card 8b)* placed a bed, a table, a chair, and a lamp in the room.

(Show 8c.) One day when Elisha was staying in that room, he asked his servant, Gehazi (Geh-hay-zye), to go and get the *(card 8b)*. Elisha said to the *(card 8b)*, "You have done so much for us," said Elisha. "Now I would like to do something for you."

Gehazi told Elisha that the *(card 8b)* and her husband had no son. So Elisha knew what he would do. "Next year at this time," he told her, "you will be carrying a *(hold up card 8d; kids say "son")* in your arms." The *(card 8b)* thought that Elisha was teasing her. But Elisha's prophecy came true, and the *(card 8b)* had a *(card 8d)*. The little boy grew up and was able to help his father work in the fields.

One day the *(card 8d)* became very sick and died. The *(card 8b)* laid her *(card 8d)* on the bed in Elisha's room and then called for her husband. She said, "Let me have one servant and a donkey. I must find Elisha, the man of God, quickly."

When Elisha saw her coming, he sent Gehazi out to meet her. But when the *(card 8b)* came close to Elisha, she got down on the ground at his feet. Gehazi tried to move her away, but Elisha stopped him. "Leave her alone! She is very upset, but God has not told me why she is upset."

The *(card 8b)* said, "Did I ask you for a *(card 8d)*?" Then Elisha realized what had happened to the boy.

Elisha called Gehazi and said, "Do not talk to anyone. Take my staff and go to the boy. Lay my staff on the boy's face." Then Gehazi left.

But the *(card 8b)* wanted Elisha to go, so Elisha went to the house of the *(card 8b)*. When he got there, the little boy was lying on his bed. Elisha went in and shut the door so he and the boy were the only ones in the room.

Elisha prayed to God. As Elisha touched the boy, he became alive again. Elisha called for Gehazi to go and get the *(card 8b)*. When she came in, Elisha said, "Take your *(card 8d)*." *(Show* Teaching Picture 8.)

When the *(card 8b)* saw what Elisha had done, she was so grateful that she fell on the ground at his feet. Then she and her *(card 8d)*, who was now alive, walked out together.

Bible Review Activity

How did God bring a boy back to life? (God worked through Elisha. Elisha touched the boy and the boy came back to life.) **Let's see what else you remember from the story.** Divide the class into four groups and give each group one of the story figures or name cards. Tell the children that you will ask questions about the story. When a question can be answered by the group's story figure or name card, that group should stand up and say "Elisha," "Gehazi," "woman," or "son." See the Review Questions for more questions.

- **I was a prophet of God.** (Elisha)
- **My husband and I built a room for Elisha.** (woman)
- **I was Elisha's servant.** (Gehazi)
- **I lived in the town of Shunem.** (woman and son)
- **I became sick and died.** (son)
- **Elisha sent me out to meet the woman.** (Gehazi)
- **I told Gehazi to go and lay my staff on the boy who had died.** (Elisha)
- **I prayed to God for the boy to get well.** (Elisha)
- **God worked through Elisha to bring me back to life.** (son)
- **I fell at Elisha's feet because my son had come back to life.** (woman)

The woman learned that God can do anything. ⌧ **We can praise God because He can do anything.**

Bible Skill Builder and Bible Memory Activity

Write "Psalm 86:9, 10" on the board. **When we want to look up something in our Bibles, we have to know several things. We need to know if it is in the Old or New Testament. Is Psalms in the Old or New Testament?** (Old) **We need to know the name of the book.** Ask a child to come to the board and point to the name of the book. (Psalm) **We need to know the chapter number.** Ask a child to point to the chapter number. (86) **We need to know the verse numbers.** Ask a child to point to the verse numbers. (9 and 10) Help the children find Psalm 86:9, 10 in their Bibles and ask for volunteers to read the verses.

Display the Bible Memory poster. Invite the children to read the verses with you while you point to the words and pictures. Then put self-stick notes over some of the words. Have kids read the poster with you again. **God is the only one worthy of our praise and worship.** ⌧ **We can praise God because He can do anything.**

Materials
Resources Sheet 5 story figures 8a and 8c and name cards 8b and 8d, CD Review Questions Unit 2 for Lesson 8 printable file

Action

Materials
white board, dry-erase marker, Bibles, *Resources* Sheet 4 Bible Memory poster, reusable adhesive, self-stick notes

Bible Skills

Added Fun!
Play "All the Nations You Have Made" from the *Resources* CD Track 7 and have kids join in.

Make It Real (15 minutes)

Step 3 • Use one of these activities to help children **identify times God has shown He can do anything.**

Materials

Activities p. 20 and corresponding stickers, colored pencils or markers

Activity Page

Teaching Tip

Be prepared to give kids ideas of what they could draw.

☰ *Quick Step* God Can Do Anything!

We've learned that God worked through Elisha to bring a boy back to life. Now let's think of other times God has shown He can do anything. Distribute the activity pages and stickers. **God can do anything!** Point to the first section. **What did God make?** (the world) Tell kids to press on the sticker of the world.

Point to the next section. **In what did God keep Noah and his family safe?** (the ark) Tell kids to press on the sticker of the ark.

What did God push back so His people could walk on dry land? (water) Tell kids to press on the sticker of water.

Who did God help David defeat? (Goliath) Tell kids to press on the sticker of Goliath. In the blank space at the bottom of the page, encourage kids to draw a picture of another time God showed He can do anything.

• **What are some other times God showed He could do anything?** (Let children share their drawings.)

Only God can do those things. God can do anything! ⊠ **We can praise God because He can do anything.**

Materials

large bag; leaf; water in a clear container; pictures of a person, the ark, and baby Jesus

Object Lesson

Option It's in the Bag

We've learned that God worked through Elisha to bring a boy back to life. Now let's think of other times God has shown He can do anything. Before class, gather the suggested items and place them in a bag. Ask for volunteers to pull out from the bag one item at a time and identify each item. Ask:

• **What does a leaf remind you of that God did?** (God made the world, including trees.) **Can anyone else make a tree?** (no)

• **What does water remind you of that God did?** (God made water. God pushed the water back so His people could cross the Red Sea on dry land.) **Can anyone else do that?** (no)

• **What does the picture of a person remind you of that God can do?** (God makes people.) **Can anyone else make people?** (no)

• **What does the ark remind you of that God did?** (God kept Noah and his family safe in the ark.) **Can anyone else do that?** (no)

• **What does the picture of baby Jesus remind you of that God did?** (God sent Jesus as a baby.) **Can anyone else do that?** (no)

Only God can do all those things. God can do anything! ⊠ **We can praise God because He can do anything.**

Materials

Weekly Bible Reader® Issue 8

Option Story from *Weekly Bible Reader®*

We've learned that God worked through Elisha to bring a boy back to life. Now let's think about other times God has shown He can do anything. Read "An Airplane Ride."

• **What are some times God has shown He can do anything?** (See the activities above for possible answers.)

Only God can do all those things. God can do anything! ⊠ **We can praise God because He can do anything.**

Step 4 • Use one of these activities to help children **praise God because He can do anything.**

≡ *Quick Step* I Praise You, God!

God can do anything! ⊠ We can praise God because He can do anything. Let's praise Him now. Tell the children that you will say things that God has done and they will respond after each thing by saying "I praise You, God. You can do anything!" On the word *God,* tell children to raise an open hand to the heavens and then downward. On the word *anything*, have them spread their arms outward. Have children stand as they praise God.

Teacher:	**You made the earth and the sky so blue.**
Children:	I praise You, God. You can do anything!
Teacher:	**You made people and animals too.**
Children:	I praise You, God. You can do anything!
Teacher:	**You kept Noah safe and the animals too.**
Children:	I praise You, God. You can do anything!
Teacher:	**You kept Moses safe when a baby so small.**
Children:	I praise You, God. You can do anything!
Teacher:	**You helped David defeat Goliath so tall.**
Children:	I praise You, God. You can do anything!
Teacher:	**You sent Jesus to earth as a baby so small.**
Children:	I praise You, God. You can do anything!
Teacher:	**I praise You, God. You can do anything!**
Children:	I praise You, God. You can do anything!

Close with a time of prayer. Encourage children to pray and praise God.

Materials

none

Option Praises

God can do anything! ⊠ We can praise God because He can do anything. We're going to praise Him now. If you did not do the first option activity in Step 3, gather the suggested items. Give each child or small group one of the items. Tell the children that they will say two sentences that praise God. For the first sentence, each child or group is to use the item given to them to come up with a sentence that praises God. The second sentence will be the same for each child or group: I praise You, God. You can do anything! (Example: Only You, God, could make a leaf. I praise You, God. You can do anything!) Help the groups with ideas only as needed.

Ask the children or groups to stand and say their praises to God. To close, lead all the children in saying "I praise You, God. You can do anything!" three times, starting loudly and getting softer each time. Close with prayer, thanking God that He can do anything.

Materials

large bag; leaf; water in a clear container; pictures of a person, the ark, and baby Jesus

Expert Tip

"Give positive rewards to those who behave or participate. Rather than focusing on the problem child, let's focus on the children who are good examples!"

—*Steve Alley*

Saying Good-bye

• Distribute Issue 8 of *Weekly Bible Reader*®.

• Make sure children have projects and activity sheets they have done.

• If you have time before parents arrive, use some of the activities on page 32.

• Remind parents that a weekly *Faith & Family* page is available online to print and use with their child at home. Go to heartshaper.com.

Evaluate

• How well did the children understand that God can do anything?

• How is your enthusiasm and joy evident to the children when you praise God?

God Heals an Obedient Naaman

Bible Focus: 2 Kings 5:1-15
Bible Memory: All the nations you have made will come and worship before you, Lord; they will bring glory to your name. For you are great and do marvelous deeds; you alone are God (Psalm 86:9, 10).
Life Focus: ⊠ We can obey God's instructions because they are right.

Heart to Heart

The Bible is a wonderful gift from God. It tells how we came into existence and how the world will end one day. It tells of heroes dying for their faith rather than giving up their faith. It also gives us instructions on how to live as God-honoring people. First John 2:3 says that "We know that we have come to know him if we obey his commands." Honor God and draw closer to Him through your obedience to His instructions.

Lesson 9 at a Glance

Step		HeartShaper Materials	Other Materials
Step 1 **Focus In** Use one of these activities to help children *explore obeying instructions.*	*Quick Step* **Who Is Obeying?** *(Activity Page)*	• *Activities* p. 21	• markers
	Option Teacher Says *(Game)*	• none	• none
	Bible Memory *Use this activity to introduce the Bible Memory verses.* *(DISCUSS)*	• none	• Bible
Step 2 **Explore His Word** Use all of these activities to help children *describe how God healed an obedient Naaman* and develop Bible skills.	**God Heals an Obedient Naaman** *(Bible Story)*	• *Resources* Sheet 5 story figures 8a, 8c, and 9b, Sheet 6 story figures 9a and 9c, CD Track 7 and Review Questions Unit 2 printable file, Sheet 4 Bible Memory poster; *Teaching Picture* 9; *Activities* p. 22	• white board, dry-erase marker, Bibles, craft sticks, clear tape, colored pencils or markers, masking tape, construction paper, paper, pencils, reusable adhesive; CD player
	Bible Review Activity *(Activity Page)*		
	Bible Skill Builder and Bible Memory Activity *(Memorize)*		
Step 3 **Make It Real** Use one of these activities to help children *discover reasons to obey God's instructions.*	*Quick Step* **Change Places!** *(Game)*	• none	• white board, dry-erase marker, paper, pencils
	Option Obey Wheels *(Discover)*	• reproducible p. 94	• scissors, paper fasteners
	Option Story from *Weekly Bible Reader®* *(LISTEN)*	• *Weekly Bible Reader®* Issue 9	• none
Step 4 **Live It Out** Use one of these activities to help children *choose to obey God's instructions.*	*Quick Step* **Take a Dip** *(Action)*	• none	• none
	Option I Will Obey You *(Pray)*	• none	• none
	Saying Good-bye	• *Weekly Bible Reader®* Issue 9	• none

Focus In (15 minutes)

Step 1 • Use one of these activities to help children **explore obeying instructions.** Use the Bible Memory activity to introduce the memory verses.

Welcome
- Welcome each child by name.
- Do check-in procedures you follow (name and security tags, offering, attendance chart, etc.).
- Early arrivers will enjoy doing one or more of the activities described on page 32.

≡ *Quick Step* Who Is Obeying?

Let's explore obeying instructions. Distribute the activity pages and markers. Read the directions aloud and do the page together.
- **Who is obeying instructions in the first row? How?**
- **What could happen if the boy never obeyed his dad's instructions?** (It might take his sister a long time to find her shoes.)
- **Who is obeying instructions in the second row? How?**
- **What could happen if the girl didn't obey her mom?** (She could run into the street and get hit by a car.)
- **Who is obeying instructions in the third row? How?**
- **What could happen if the girl never obeyed her teacher?** (She might never take the time to pray to God.)
- **Who are some people who give instructions you need to obey?** (parents, grandparents, teachers, coaches, and so forth)
- **What are some instructions your parents ask you to obey?**

There are lots of instructions we need to obey. We are going to learn that ⊠ we can obey God's instructions because they are right.

Materials
Activities p. 21, markers

Activity Page

Added Fun!
Let children take turns naming instructions. The rest of the class can decide who would give each instruction.

Option Teacher Says

Let's explore obeying instructions as we play a fun game. Tell the children that you will give some instructions. They are only to obey those instructions that you begin by saying "teacher says." If they obey an instruction when you don't say "teacher says," they are out of the game. The following are some examples:

Teacher says to clap three times. Jump up and down five times. Teacher says to hop on one foot. Stop hopping on one foot. Now twirl around three times. Teacher says to pat your head six times. Teacher says to stomp your foot one time. Now stomp your foot four times.
- **Who are some people who give instructions you need to obey?** (parents, grandparents, teachers, coaches, and so forth)
- **What are some instructions your parents ask you to obey?**

There are lots of instructions we need to obey. We are going to learn that ⊠ we can obey God's instructions because they are right.

Materials
none

Game

Bible Memory Psalm 86:9, 10

Divide the class into two groups. Read aloud Psalm 86:9, 10. Alternate between the two groups as you ask these questions: **Who made all the nations?** (God) **What will all the nations do?** (worship God) **Who will bring glory to God's name?** (all the nations) **Who is great?** (God) **Who does marvelous deeds?** (God) **How many Gods are there?** (one) **These verses have helped us learn a lot about God. We're also going to learn that ⊠ we can obey God's instructions because they are right.**

Materials
Bible

Transition to Explore His Word
See the *Resources* CD Transition Tips printable file. As children gather, make sure you have all the materials you need.

Explore His Word (20 minutes)

Step 2 • Use all of these activities to help children **describe how God healed an obedient Naaman** and develop Bible skills.

Bible Background for the Teacher

Naaman, a successful Aramean army commander, had leprosy. Leprosy, today known as Hansen's disease, was a prevalent but devastating skin disease in Bible times. Leprosy is characterized by spreading spots, nodules, and open sores that ultimately results in loss of feeling, paralysis, and deformity (see Leviticus 13, 14). The term *leprosy* can also be used generically to refer to various skin diseases.

Aram and the northern kingdom had made a treaty during the days of Israel's King Ahab (1 Kings 20:34). However, bands of Arameans still made raids across the border into Israel. Naaman's slave girl came into his possession as a result of one such raid.

Aram's king sent a letter to Israel's king, erroneously assuming that Elisha was under the command of the king. Likewise, Israel's king erroneously assumed that the king of Aram was looking for an excuse to make war.

Naaman was angered both by the message and by the messenger (Elisha's servant instead of Elisha). Yet Naaman's high-ranking status hadn't kept him from getting leprosy, nor could it keep him from needing to humbly accept the way to healing that God provided.

When Naaman came up out of the Jordan the seventh time, he was healed—both physically and spiritually, testifying, "Now I know that there is no God in all the world except in Israel" (2 Kings 5:15).

Worship Time

If you want to offer a time of worship, see the *Resources* CD Worship Time Ideas printable file for suggestions.

Materials

white board; dry-erase marker; Bibles; *Resources* Sheet 5 story figures 8a, 8c, and 9b, Sheet 6 story figures 9a and 9c; craft sticks; clear tape; *Teaching Picture* 9 (optional: poster board and reusable adhesive)

Before Class

Attach story figures 9a and 9c back-to-back on a craft stick. You may want to attach the river figure, 9b, to a piece of poster board.

God Heals an Obedient Naaman   (2 Kings 5:1-15)

Our Bible story comes once again from the Old Testament book of 2 Kings. Write "2 Kings 5:1" on the board. Point to the Scripture reference as you talk about it. **The name of the book is ___** (invite children to respond together). **The chapter number is ___. The verse number is ___.** Help children turn to 2 Kings 5:1. Ask for a volunteer to read the first part of the verse.

Help me tell today's Bible story. When you hear a number, count quickly to that number. And you need to listen for how God healed an obedient man. Hold up the story figures as indicated during the story.

(Show 9a.) A man named Naaman *(Nay-uh-mun)* was a very important man. He was the commander of the army of the king of Aram. He was mighty and brave. He had won many battles, and the king of Aram liked him. But Naaman had a skin disease called leprosy. It was a terrible disease that no doctor could cure.

One *(kids count to one)* little servant girl from the land of Israel lived and worked at Naaman's house. She was concerned about Naaman. She told Naaman's wife about a prophet of God who could make Naaman well.

When Naaman heard this news, he went to the king of Aram and asked if he could go and see this prophet. So the king gave him a letter to take to the king of Israel, where the prophet lived.

Naaman gave the king of Israel the letter. The king of Israel became very upset. He couldn't make sick people better! He thought his enemies were playing a bad trick on him to get his army to fight.

(Show 8a.) But a prophet of God named Elisha heard about the problem and sent word to the king to send Naaman to Elisha. Finally Naaman would get to see the prophet! But before Naaman could even get into Elisha's home, Elisha's servant came out with a message *(show 8c)*. "Elisha says if you go and wash in the Jordan River **seven** *(kids count)* times, you will be healed."

Naaman could not believe what he was hearing! He had come all this way, and Elisha had sent a servant to speak to him. The Jordan River was not a very good river anyway, and Naaman became very angry. He turned around to go back home.

Naaman's servants wanted him to get well. "If he had asked you to do something hard, you would have done it," they said. "Why can't you obey what Elisha said to do? This very simple thing might heal your skin." Naaman realized his servants were right.

Naaman went to the Jordan River *(show 9b)* and stepped into the water. He dipped himself into the water **one** time and came up. He still had leprosy. Elisha's servant had said **seven** times, so Naaman went down and came up again—**two, three, four, five, six,** and **seven.** Naaman obeyed and did exactly what Elisha had told him to do. The servants watched as Naaman went down for the **seventh** time and came up out of the water. *(Show* Teaching Picture *9.)*

When Naaman looked at himself, he was clean and well! *(Turn 9a around to show 9c.)* His skin no longer had the terrible sores of leprosy! It looked like the soft, clear skin of a little boy! Naaman went back to Elisha and said, "Now I know that there is no God in all the world except in Israel" (v. 15).

Bible Review Activity

How did God heal Naaman? (Naaman obeyed what Elisha's servant had told him to do. He dipped himself in the Jordan River seven times.) **Let's see what else you remember from the story.** Distribute the activity pages and colored pencils or markers. Read the directions aloud and do the page together.

As time permits, play a review game using the Review Questions. Using masking tape, make a large tic-tac-toe grid on the floor. Divide the class into two teams. Give each team several sheets of the same color of construction paper. Alternate asking the teams questions. When a team answers a question correctly, a child from that team can hold a sheet of construction paper and stand in one of the grids. Keep playing until a team gets three in a row.

Naaman obeyed the instructions and was healed of his leprosy. God has given us instructions to obey too. We're learning that ⊠ we can obey God's instructions because they are right.

Bible Skill Builder and Bible Memory Activity

Psalm 86:9 and 10 are the Bible Memory verses we have been learning. Write "Psalm 86:9, 10" on the board. Distribute paper and pencils. Tell the children to copy the Scripture reference on their papers. Ask kids to draw a box around the name of the book, a circle around the chapter number, and a triangle around the verse number. **Everyone, call out the answers: What is the name of the book?** (Psalms) **What is the chapter number?** (86) **What are the verse numbers?** (9 and 10) Help children look up Psalm 86:9, 10. Ask for volunteers to read the verses.

Display the Bible Memory poster and read the verses together. Then remove the poster and lead the kids in saying the verses together. Give time for those children who would like to say the verses by themselves. Play "All the Nations You Have Made" from the CD and encourage kids to join in.

Because God is great and is the only God, ⊠ we can obey God's instructions because they are right.

Make It Real (15 minutes)

Step 3 • Use one of these activities to help children **discover reasons to obey God's instructions.**

Materials
white board, dry-erase marker, paper, pencils

Added Fun!
After a couple of rounds, have kids exchange papers and continue playing.

Materials
reproducible p. 94, scissors, paper fasteners

Teaching Tips
You may want to pair advanced readers with less advanced readers.

Copying the page onto card stock will make the wheels and arrows more durable. Kids might also enjoy decorating their wheels with markers.

Materials
Weekly Bible Reader®
Issue 9

≡ *Quick Step* Change Places!

We've learned that Naaman obeyed Elisha's instructions and was healed of leprosy. God has given us instructions to obey too. What are some reasons we should obey God's instructions? As children give reasons, list them on the board. (God loves us. God wants us to obey. God knows what is best for us. God's instructions are good. We obey because we love God. We obey because we want to please God.) Distribute the paper and pencils. Ask kids to write on their papers one of the reasons to obey God.

Ask the children to hold their papers and sit in a circle. You can stand in the middle of the circle. Call out two of the reasons to obey God's instructions and then say "Change places!" The children who have those reasons written on their papers are to change places with each other before you (or the person in the middle) can sit in one of their places. Whoever is left without a place to sit can be in the middle and call out two other reasons to obey God's instructions. Play as time permits.

There are lots of reasons to obey God's instructions. ☒ We can obey God's instructions because they are right.

Option   Obey Wheels

We've learned that Naaman obeyed Elisha's instructions and was healed of leprosy. God has given us instructions to obey too. Let's discover reasons to obey God's instructions. Before class, make copies of the reproducible page. Distribute the reproducible pages, scissors, and paper fasteners. Have the children cut out the wheels and the arrows and attach the arrows with paper fasteners to the wheels. Tell kids that the sentences on the wheel tell reasons to obey God's instructions. Ask for volunteers to read the sentences aloud. Tell the children that you will name some of God's instructions. They are to place their arrow on a reason to obey each instruction. After each instruction, ask a few kids to share where they placed their arrows.

Instructions: **Obey your parents. Tell the truth. Help others. Share with others. Keep your promises. Love others. Go to church services. Do not steal. Don't use God's name in vain. Treat others how you want to be treated. Worship God. Always put God first.**

There are lots of reasons to obey God's instructions. ☒ We can obey God's instructions because they are right.

Option   Story from *Weekly Bible Reader*®

We've learned that Naaman obeyed Elisha's instructions and was healed of leprosy. God has given us instructions to obey too. Let's discover reasons to obey God's instructions. Read "God Is Watching."

• **What are some reasons to obey God's instructions?** (See activities above.)

There are lots of reasons to obey God's instructions. ☒ We can obey God's instructions because they are right.

Step 4 • Use one of these activities to help children **choose to obey God's instructions.**

≡ *Quick Step* Take a Dip

Materials
none

We've learned that there are lots of reasons to obey God's instructions. And we know that ⊠ we can obey God's instructions because they are right. Now *you* need to choose to obey God's instructions. Ask kids to stand in a circle. Tell the children that you will name some of God's instructions. When they hear one of God's instructions they choose to obey, they can pretend to be Naaman and "dip into the water." If a child doesn't choose to obey an instruction, don't point it out or belittle the child.

Instructions: **Obey your parents.** Pause between each instruction. **Tell the truth. Help others. Share with others. Keep your promises. Love others. Go to church services. Do not steal. Don't use God's name in vain. Treat others how you want to be treated. Worship God. Always put God first.**

Close with a time of prayer. Encourage children to pray and ask for God's help in obeying His instructions.

Option   I Will Obey You

Materials
none

We've learned that there are lots of reasons to obey God's instructions. And we know that ⊠ we can obey God's instructions because they are right. Now *you* need to choose to obey God's instructions. Have the children gather for a time of prayer. Tell the children that you will pray sentence prayers about obeying God's instructions. If they choose to obey an instruction, they should silently pray the same prayer.

Dear God, I will obey You by obeying my parents. Pause after each sentence prayer so children can pray silently. **I will obey You by telling the truth. I will obey You by sharing with others. I will obey You by loving others. I will obey You by not stealing. I will obey You by worshiping You. I will obey You by always putting You first. In Jesus' name, amen.**

Saying Good-bye

Evaluate
• What did the children say or do to indicate they understand the need to obey God's instructions?
• What actions do you need to take to help children better obey the classroom rules?

• Distribute Issue 9 of *Weekly Bible Reader*® and the *Activities* page 11 Unit 2 Bible Memory poster and stickers if you have not already done so.

• Make sure children have projects and activity sheets they have done.

• If you have time before parents arrive, use some of the activities on page 32.

• Remind parents that a weekly *Faith & Family* page is available online to print and use with their child at home. Go to heartshaper.com.

Unit 3

	Bible Focus	**Life Focus**
Lesson 10 Solomon Prays for Wisdom	God hears Solomon's prayer. 1 Kings 3, 4	☒ God hears our prayers to make right choices.
Lesson 11 Hezekiah Prays for Healing	God hears Hezekiah's prayer. 2 Kings 20	☒ God hears our prayers when we are sick.
Lesson 12 Jehoshaphat Prays for Help	God hears Jehoshaphat's prayer. 2 Chronicles 20	☒ God hears our prayers when we need help.
Lesson 13 Manasseh Prays for Forgiveness	God hears Manasseh's prayer. 2 Chronicles 33	☒ God hears our prayers when we need forgiveness.

Bible Memory

1 Thessalonians 5:16-18

Rejoice always; pray continually; give thanks in all circumstances, for this is God's will for you in Christ Jesus.

Print the KJV or NIV Additional Bible Memory file from the Resources CD for more Bible Memory verses kids will enjoy learning.

Bible Skill for Unit 3

Children will

- name Old Testament main characters.

Ongoing Bible Skills

Children will

- find verses in the Bible.
- begin to read Bible verses.
- memorize selected Bible verses.

Life Skills for Unit 3

Children will

- desire to pray to God.
- thank God for His help and forgiveness.
- choose to pray for others.

HeartShaper Materials for Unit 3

Early Elementary Activities, Lessons 10–13 and the Unit 3 Bible Memory Poster and Stickers

Early Elementary Teaching Pictures, Lessons 10–13

Early Elementary Resources

CD

"Be Joyful Always," Tracks 3, 4

"Show My Love," Tracks 5, 6

Bible Story for Lesson 11, Track 10

Bible Memory: *KJV or NIV* Additional Bible Memory for Unit 3, *New International Version* Bible Memory for Unit 3, *King James Version* Bible Memory for Unit 3

Bible Skills Worksheets, Unit 3

Buzzy Bee Letters, Lessons 10–13

Worship Time Ideas, Unit 3

Review Questions, Unit 3

Letter to Families, Unit 3

Posters and Activities: Books of the Old Testament posters, Books of the New Testament posters

Teacher Helps: Attendance Chart, Discipline and Classroom Management, Early Elementary Children, Leading Young Hearts Guide, Safety and Security Issues, Starting the New Year, Transition Tips, Easels and Supports

Visuals

Sheet 6 Bible Memory shapes and photo cards; Sheet 7 crown and story props 10a–10c, 11a–11d, 12a–12c, 13a–13d, and situation cards; Sheet 8 game board and cards

Weekly Bible Reader® Issues 10–13 and the Special Issue

Faith & Family online resource

A weekly devotional guide for parents and kids to use together. Go to heartshaper.com.

Additional Activities for Unit 3

Use these activities for early arrivers, for children who finish activities quickly, and when you are waiting for parents to arrive.

"A Flock of Thankful Prayers" Bulletin Board

Cut letters for the title and mount them across the top of the board. Print Psalm 95:2a on colorful paper and attach it to the board. Enlarge the turkey pattern in the narrow column and make a copy for each child. Encourage kids to write prayers of thanks on the turkeys. Then they can color the turkeys, cut them out, and attach them to the bulletin board.

Prayer Box

Provide a small box with a separate lid. Let kids decorate the box and the lid. Provide index cards and pencils. One week, have the kids write prayer requests on the cards (or draw pictures). During your prayer time, read the requests and pray about them. Another week, have the kids write (or draw) things to thank God for. During your prayer time, give thanks for the things kids mentioned on their cards. For another week, kids could write the names of people who are sick, and for the other week, kids could write their prayers to God.

Cards of Thanksgiving

Provide supplies so kids can make thank-you cards for family members, teachers, and others. They could say thanks for loving them, taking care of them, teaching them, and so forth.

Prayer Cups Craft

Cut light-colored construction paper into small rectangles, approximately 2" x 3". Give each child four cards. Write on the board "Pray about making right choices," "Pray for healing," "Pray for help," and "Pray for forgiveness." Tell children to write the sentences on the cards. Let children decorate foam or paper cups with markers and stickers. They can place the cards inside the cups. Tell the kids to pull the cards out of the cup as reminders of things they can pray about.

Bible Skills

Make copies of the Bible Skills Worksheets for Unit 3 from the *Resources* CD. For Unit 3, children will name Old Testament main characters.

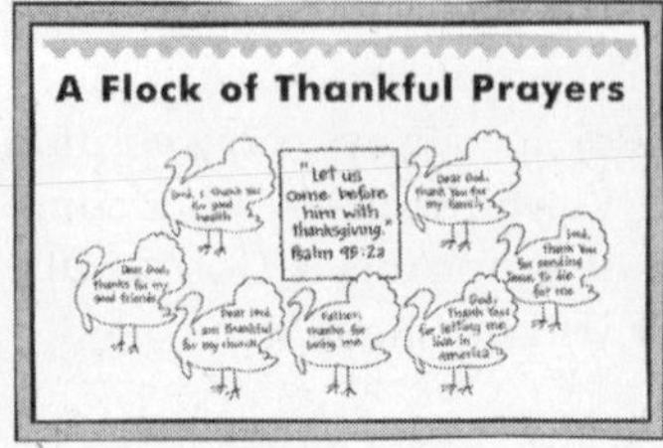

Solomon Prays for Wisdom

10

Bible Focus: 1 Kings 3:4-14; 4:29-34
Bible Memory: Rejoice always; pray continually; give thanks in all circumstances, for this is God's will for you in Christ Jesus (1 Thessalonians 5:16-18).
Life Focus: ⌧ God hears our prayers to make right choices.

Heart to Heart

Take some time to reflect about the prayers you offer to God. Do you thank God and praise Him often in your prayers? Do you tell God you love Him? Do you ask for forgiveness? Do you pray for others? Hopefully you can answer yes to those questions. Do you often pray selfishly? Do you pray and ask God to take revenge on those who have hurt or disappointed you? Hopefully you can answer no to those questions.

Prayer is a simple thing and yet a very powerful thing. Prayer will draw you and keep you close to God. Pray for God's help in making right choices—He will answer.

Lesson 10 at a Glance

		HeartShaper Materials	Other Materials
Step 1 **Focus In** Use one of these activities to help children *discover what prayer is.*	*Quick Step* **What Is Prayer?** *Activity Page*	• *Activities* p. 24	• pencils
	Option Prayer Is, Prayer Isn't *Action*	• none	• index cards, marker, paper, reusable adhesive or pushpins
	Bible Memory *Use this activity to introduce the Bible Memory verses.* *DISCUSS*	• none	• Bible
Step 2 **Explore His Word** Use all of these activities to help children *tell what Solomon prayed for and how God answered his prayer* and develop Bible skills.	**Solomon Prays for Wisdom** *Bible Story*	• *Resources* Sheet 7 crown, Solomon's name 10a and story props 10b and 10c, Sheet 6 Bible Memory shapes, CD Review Questions Unit 3 printable file; *Teaching Picture* 10; *Activities* p. 23	• white board, dry-erase marker, Bibles, clear tape, reusable adhesive, pencils or markers
	Bible Review Activity *Game*		
	Bible Skill Builder and Bible Memory Activity *Bible Skills*		
Step 3 **Make It Real** Use one of these activities to help children *discuss the need to pray about making right choices.*	*Quick Step* **Choices, Choices** *DISCUSS*	• *Resources* Sheet 6 photo cards	• none
	Option Making Right Choices *Act It Out*	• none	• paper, pen
	Option Story from *Weekly Bible Reader®* *LISTEN*	• *Weekly Bible Reader®* Issue 10	• none
Step 4 **Live It Out** Use one of these activities to help children *pray about making right choices.*	*Quick Step* **Help Us Choose** *Pray*	• *Resources* Sheet 6 photo cards	• none
	Option Prayer Pennants *Craft*	• reproducible p. 95	• markers, scissors, straws or craft sticks, clear tape
	Saying Good-bye	• *Weekly Bible Reader®* Issue 10 and the Special Issue, *Activities* p. 31 Unit 3 Bible Memory poster and stickers	• none

Life Focus
⌧ God hears our prayers to make right choices.

Step 1 • Use one of these activities to help children **discover what prayer is.** Use the Bible Memory activity to introduce the memory verses.

Welcome
- Welcome each child by name.
- Do check-in procedures you follow (name and security tags, offering, attendance chart, etc.).
- Early arrivers will enjoy doing one or more of the activities described on page 64.

Quick Step What Is Prayer?

Let's think about prayer and discover what prayer is. Distribute the activity pages and pencils. Read the directions aloud and do the page together. Have children show thumbs-up when a sentence tells what the Bible says about prayer. Have children show thumbs-down when a sentence does not tell what the Bible says about prayer. Ask for a volunteer to read the first sentence aloud. Children should show thumbs-up. Ask for volunteers to read the other sentences and give time for kids to respond. The children should show thumbs-down and cross out the third and fifth sentences.
- **What is prayer?** (talking to God)
- **When can you pray to God?** (bedtime, before meals, anytime)
- **What are some things you can say to God in prayer?** (thank God, tell God I love Him, ask for forgiveness, pray for others)

There are a lot of things we can say to God in prayer. Today we're going to discover that ⌧ God hears our prayers to make right choices.

Materials
Activities p. 24, pencils

Activity Page

Expert Tip
"Remove distractions and keep the children focused. Be prepared. And remember, your lesson begins when the first student arrives!"
—*Steven James*

Option Prayer Is, Prayer Isn't

Let's discover what prayer is. Before class, write on separate index cards some things prayer is and some things prayer is not (see the narrow column). Make two signs, "Prayer Is" and "Prayer Is Not," and place the signs side-by-side on a wall or bulletin board.

Give each child (or pair or small group of children) one of the index cards. Tell kids that some of the cards have sentences that tell what prayer is and some have sentences that tell what prayer isn't. Children are to read their cards and attach their cards under the correct sign. When all the cards are in place, read the sentences aloud and ask the kids if they think the cards are in the right column.
- **What is prayer?** (talking to God)
- **What are some things you can say to God in prayer?** (thank God, tell God I love Him, ask for forgiveness, pray for others)

There are a lot of things we can say to God in prayer. Today we're going to discover that ⌧ God hears our prayers to make right choices.

Materials
index cards, marker, paper, reusable adhesive or pushpins

Action

For Index Cards
Prayer is talking to God. God hears our prayers. We can only pray at bedtime. We can pray anytime. We have to be in a church building to pray. When we pray, we can thank God. The Bible tells us to never stop praying. When we pray, we can pray for others.

Bible Memory 1 Thessalonians 5:16-18

Select three children and quietly tell them each to pose in one of the following ways: kneeling, sitting with hands folded, or standing with head bowed and eyes shut. **What do you think these kids are doing?** (praying) **To whom do we talk when we pray?** (God) **Do we have to be in one of these positions when we pray?** (no) Read 1 Thessalonians 5:16-18 aloud. **Our new Bible Memory verses tell us some things about prayer. We're going to discover that ⌧ God hears our prayers to make right choices.**

Materials
Bible

Transition to Explore His Word
See the *Resources* CD Transition Tips printable file. As children gather, make sure you have all the materials you need.

Explore His Word (20 minutes)

Step 2 • Use all of these activities to help children **tell what Solomon prayed for and how God answered his prayer** and develop Bible skills.

Bible Background for the Teacher

During the early part of his reign, King Solomon, son and successor of King David, went to Gibeon, a city northwest of Jerusalem. At Gibeon, Solomon earnestly sought the Lord's favor by sacrificing 1,000 burnt offerings. God appeared to Solomon in a dream and told him to ask for whatever he wanted.

Such an offer would be hard for anyone to wisely answer, let alone someone Solomon's age. Solomon was probably about 20 years old. Solomon's conversation with God, however, indicates an enormous amount of maturity. God responded positively to Solomon's humble prayer. God not only gave Solomon that for which he asked but also the many good things for which he didn't ask. This illustrates the principle that Jesus later speaks of in Matthew 6:33 and Luke 12:31 regarding the rewards of seeking God's kingdom before personal gain.

King Solomon's wisdom extended far beyond his ability to govern his kingdom and also included insight into natural sciences. He was wiser than anyone prior to Jesus (Luke 11:31). Solomon is credited with writing the Old Testament books of Ecclesiastes, most of Proverbs, and Song of Songs (also known as Song of Solomon).

Worship Time

If you want to offer a time of worship, see the *Resources* CD Worship Time Ideas printable file for suggestions.

Materials

white board; dry-erase marker; Bibles; *Resources* Sheet 7 crown, Solomon's name 10a and story props 10b, 10c; *Teaching Picture* 10; clear tape; reusable adhesive

Before Class

Prepare the crown. Tape the three strips together and tape to the sides of the headpiece. Adjust to fit as necessary. Place 10a on the crown with reusable adhesive.

Solomon Prays for Wisdom (1 Kings 3:4-14; 4:29-34)

Let's think about some people from the Old Testament whom we have learned about. Have we learned about David? (yes) **Who did David play the harp for?** (King Saul) **Who did David defeat?** (Goliath) **Who was David's good friend?** (Jonathan) **Our Bible story comes from the Old Testament book of 1 Kings.** Write "1 Kings 3:4" on the board. **In the book of 1 Kings, we learn about men who were kings. Today we are going to learn about King Solomon, the son of King David.** Help children find 1 Kings 3:4 in their Bibles and ask for a volunteer to read the first part of the verse.

You can help tell today's Bible story. Hold up the 10c wisdom card. **When you see this card, say "wisdom."** Hold up the crown. **When you see this crown, say "King Solomon."** Practice these with the children. **You also need to listen for what Solomon prayed for and how God answered his prayer.**

King Solomon went to the city of Gibeon to worship God. He wanted to serve God like his father King David had done. *(Hold up the crown; kids say "King Solomon")* wanted to be a good leader. While he was there, God came to Solomon in a dream during the night. God said, "Ask for whatever you want. I will give it to you."

Would *(hold up the crown; kids say "King Solomon")* ask God for money *(show 10b)*? Would he ask for a great palace? Would Solomon ask for beautiful jewelry? Would he ask to become famous? Solomon answered God, "You have been very kind to my father and me. I ask for *(hold up wisdom card; kids say "wisdom")* so I'll know how to rule your people. Help me know the difference between right and wrong. I want to rule your people in the right way."

This pleased God very much. God said to *(hold up the crown; kids say "King Solomon")*, "You did not ask for riches so you could be wealthy *(show 10b)*. And you did not ask for a long life. Since you asked to be able to choose right and make wise decisions, I will give you what you asked. I will give you *(hold up wisdom card; kids say "wisdom")* to help you do right and make right choices. You will be wiser than anyone. And I will give you riches *(show 10b)* and honor and a long life too."

(Hold up the crown; kids say "King Solomon") was known everywhere for being wise. He was wiser than anyone in the entire world. God gave Solomon the ability to make good decisions and right choices. Solomon wrote 3,000 wise sayings, which we have in our Bible in the book of Proverbs. He also taught about plants, animals, birds, and fish. People came from all over the world to hear Solomon talk about these things. *(Show Teaching Picture 10.)*

Solomon asked God for *(hold up wisdom card; kids say "wisdom")*. And God made Solomon very wise. But God also gave Solomon even more than he asked for. He gave *(hold up the crown; kids say "King Solomon")* riches and honor and a long life.

Bible Review Activity

What did Solomon pray for? (wisdom) **How did God answer his prayer?** (by making him wiser than anyone and giving him riches, honor, and a long life) **Let's see what else you remember from the Bible story.** Distribute the activity pages and pencils or markers. Read the directions aloud and do the page together. (Questions 1, 2, 4, 5 are true; 3 and 6 are false.)

Then have the children gather in a circle to play this game. Tell the kids that they will pass the crown around the circle until you say "King Solomon." Whoever is holding the crown should put it on while you ask her a question about the Bible story. For more questions, see the Review Questions on the CD.

• **Who was King Solomon's father?** (David)
• **Who told Solomon to ask for whatever he wanted?** (God)
• **What did Solomon ask God for?** (wisdom to rule God's people)
• **How did God feel about Solomon's request?** (It pleased Him.)
• **Who was Solomon wiser than?** (everyone in the world)
• **Who came to hear Solomon's wise teachings?** (people from all over the world)

Solomon made the right choice when he asked God for wisdom and God heard and answered Solomon's prayer. We're going to discover that ⊠ God hears our prayers to make right choices too.

Bible Skill Builder and Bible Memory Activity

The Bible is divided into two main sections, the Old Testament and the New Testament. Find the table of contents near the front of your Bibles. Write "1 Thessalonians 5:16-18" on the board. Ask kids to point to the New Testament section and then run their fingers down the list until they find the book of 1 Thessalonians. Tell kids to find the page number 1 Thessalonians begins on and turn to it. Help them find chapter 5, verses 16-18. Ask for volunteers to read the verses.

Before class, press out the Bible Memory shapes. Attach them vertically or horizontally to a wall or bulletin board. Show kids the Bible Memory shapes. Read the verses aloud while pointing to the words. Ask kids to join you in reading the verses while you point to the words. Then remove the Bible Memory shapes from the wall and give a shape to each child. Tell kids that they are to line up so that the words are in order. Or they can lay the shapes on a table and put them in order. Help as needed. When kids have lined up the shapes correctly, applaud their efforts.

Our Bible Memory verses tell us that we are to pray all the time and to give thanks when we pray. And, just like King Solomon, ⊠ God hears our prayers to make right choices.

Make It Real (15 minutes)

Step 3 • Use one of these activities to help children **discuss the need to pray about making right choices.**

Materials
Resources Sheet 6 photo cards

Photo Pairs
apple and french fries, flash cards and catcher's mitt, sponges and cups and saucers and bicycle, girl with umbrella and girl sharing umbrella

Materials
paper, pen

Materials
Weekly Bible Reader®
Issue 10

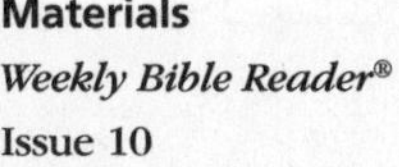

≡ *Quick Step* Choices, Choices

We've discovered that Solomon made the right choice when he asked God for wisdom. Let's think about why we need to pray and ask God to help us make right choices. Give each child (or pair or small group of children) one set of the photo pairs.

Ask the children with the french fries and apple, **You have a choice: eat french fries or an apple. What is the more healthy choice?**

Ask the children with the catcher's mitt and the flash cards, **You have a choice: study for a test or play softball. What is the right choice?**

Ask the children with the sponges and cups and saucers and bicycle, **You have a choice: help wash the dishes or ride your bicycle. What is the right choice?**

Ask the children with the girl with the umbrella and the girl sharing the umbrella, **You have a choice: share your umbrella or don't share it. What is the right choice?**

• **Is it always easy to make right choices?** (no)
• **Who can help us make right choices?** (God)
• **How do we ask for God's help?** (pray)

There are a lot of choices we make every day, and we need God's help to make right choices. ⊠ **God hears our prayers to make right choices.**

Option Making Right Choices

We've discovered that Solomon made the right choice when he asked God for wisdom. Let's think about why we need to pray and ask God to help us make right choices. Before class, write the following on separate slips of paper:

1. You have a spelling test tomorrow that you need to study for, but you want to play with your friends. 2. Your parents asked you to clean your room, but you would rather play a game. 3. Your mom asked you not to eat any more cookies, but you really want to. 4. Your teacher asked you to help the new girl in school with homework, but you don't want to. 5. Your parents told you it's time for bed, but you don't want to go to bed.

Have children act out the situations, asking others to help as needed. After each situation, ask:

• **What is the wrong choice to make?**
• **What is the right choice to make?**
• **Who can help you make the right choice?** (God)
• **How do you ask for God's help?** (pray)

There are a lot of choices we make every day, and we need God's help to make right choices. ⊠ **God hears our prayers to make right choices.**

Option Story from *Weekly Bible Reader*®

We've discovered that Solomon made the right choice when he asked God for wisdom. Let's think about why we need to pray and ask God to help us make right choices. Read "Birthday Money."

There are a lot of choices we make every day, and we need God's help to make right choices. ⊠ **God hears our prayers to make right choices.**

Live It Out (10 minutes)

Step 4 • Use one of these activities to help children **pray about making right choices.**

≡ *Quick Step* Help Us Choose

We know that there are lots of choices we make every day and that we need God's help in making the right choices. It's good to know that ⊠ God hears our prayers to make right choices. Have the children gather for a prayer circle.

Hold up the apple and french fries photo cards. Ask for a volunteer to pray and ask God to help us make the right choice to eat healthy foods.

Hold up the flash cards and catcher's mitt photo cards. Ask for a volunteer to pray and ask God to help us make the right choice to study and do our schoolwork.

Hold up the sponges and cups and saucers and the bicycle photo cards. Ask for a volunteer to pray and ask God to help us make the right choice to work hard at the jobs we do at home.

Hold up the girl sharing the umbrella and the girl not sharing the umbrella. Ask for a volunteer to pray and ask God to help us make the right choice to share.

Close the prayer time by thanking God for His help in making the right choices.

Option Prayer Pennants

We know that there are lots of choices we make every day and that we need God's help in making the right choices. It's good to know that ⊠ God hears our prayers to make right choices. Before class, make copies of the reproducible page. Distribute the reproducible pages, markers, scissors, straws or craft sticks, and clear tape. The children can choose one or both of the pennants to make. They are to color the pennants, cut them out, and attach to straws or craft sticks. **Put your pennants where you will see them and be reminded that ⊠ God hears our prayers to make right choices.**

After children have completed the pennants, lead the children in a time of directed prayer. Tell the children that you will give them some ideas of things to pray about and they are to pray silently. **Dear God, help us to make right choices. (pause) Help us to make the right choice to share with others. (pause) Help us to make the right choice to work hard at the jobs we do at home. (pause) Help us to make the right choice to study and do our schoolwork. (pause) Help us to make the choice to eat healthy foods. (pause) God, thank You for hearing our prayers to make right choices. In Jesus' name, amen.**

Saying Good-bye

• Distribute Issue 10 and the Special Issue of *Weekly Bible Reader*® and the *Activities* page 31 Unit 3 Bible Memory poster and stickers. Encourage kids to complete their posters at home by adding the stickers.

• Make sure children have projects and activity sheets they have done.

• If you have time before parents arrive, use some of the activities on page 64.

• Remind parents that a weekly *Faith & Family* page is available online to print and use with their child at home. Go to heartshaper.com.

Materials
Resources Sheet 6
photo cards

Added Fun!
Play "Show My Love" from the *Resources* CD Tracks 5 and 6 and invite kids to join in singing to thank God for hearing our prayers.

Materials
reproducible p. 95, markers, scissors, straws or craft sticks, clear tape

Evaluate
• How did the children demonstrate they are beginning to understand about prayer?

• Which children are not comfortable praying aloud? How can you help them?

Hezekiah Prays for Healing

Bible Focus: 2 Kings 20:1-11
Bible Memory: Rejoice always; pray continually; give thanks in all circumstances, for this is God's will for you in Christ Jesus (1 Thessalonians 5:16-18).
Life Focus: ☒ God hears our prayers when we are sick.

Heart to Heart

Just like many of us, Hezekiah cried out to God when he was ill. Sickness and disease strike every family, some more so than others. The prayer lists in church bulletins and newsletters show that Christians believe God will hear and answer prayers for healing.

But have you ever been a part of a prayer gathering or a small group and all the prayers were for healing of one kind or another? Surely God never intended for all of our prayers to be for healing. Take time to think about your prayers. Be sure to pray for those who are sick, but remember that there are lots of other things to talk to God about too.

Lesson 11 at a Glance

Step 1 **Focus In** Use one of these activities to help children *explore being sick*.	*Quick Step* **The Faces of Sickness** 	**HeartShaper Materials** • none	**Other Materials** • paper or paper plates, markers
	Option Doctor on Call 	• none	• bandage wraps; adhesive bandages; toy stethoscope, blood pressure cuff, etc.
	Bible Memory  *Use this activity to introduce the Bible Memory verses.*	• *Resources* Sheet 6 Bible Memory shapes	• Bible, reusable adhesive or pushpins
Step 2 **Explore His Word** Use all of these activities to help children *tell what Hezekiah prayed for and how God answered his prayer* and develop Bible skills.	**Hezekiah Prays for Healing**  **Bible Review Activity**  **Bible Skill Builder and Bible Memory Activity** 	• *Resources* Sheet 7 crown, Hezekiah's name 11a, story props 11b–11d, CD Review Questions Unit 3 printable file and Tracks 3 and 4; *Teaching Picture* 11	• white board, dry-erase marker, Bibles, reusable adhesive, CD player
Step 3 **Make It Real** Use one of these activities to help children *explain why it's important to pray for people who are sick*.	*Quick Step* **Praying Hands Game** 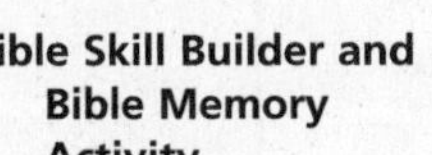	• none	• white board, dry-erase marker, construction paper, markers
	Option Rising Prayers 	• none	• water in a transparent glass or jar, permanent marker, effervescent antacid tablet
	Option Story from *Weekly Bible Reader®*	• *Weekly Bible Reader®* Issue 11	• none
Step 4 **Live It Out** Use one of these activities to help children *pray for someone who is sick*.	*Quick Step* **Get Well Soon!** 	• *Activities* p. 25 and corresponding stickers	• markers or colored pencils, scissors, glue
	Option Prayer Journal 	• none	• paper, markers, white board, dry-erase marker
	Saying Good-bye	• *Weekly Bible Reader®* Issue 11	• none

Life Focus
⊠ God hears our prayers when we are sick.

Step 1 • Use one of these activities to help children **explore being sick.** Use the Bible Memory activity to introduce the memory verses.

Welcome
- Welcome each child by name.
- Do check-in procedures you follow (name and security tags, offering, attendance chart, etc.).
- Early arrivers will enjoy doing one or more of the activities described on page 64.

≡ *Quick Step* The Faces of Sickness

Let's explore being sick. Have you ever been sick? Allow a few children to share their stories about being sick. **How do you feel when you are sick?** (tired, yucky, stomach hurts, head hurts, in pain, throat hurts) Distribute the paper plates and markers. **Draw faces to show how you feel when you are sick.** After kids are done, allow them to share their drawings.

- **What do people do to try to get well?** (go to a doctor, take medicine, go to a hospital, rest, sleep, drink juice)
- **Who helps us when we are sick?** (moms and dads, other family members, doctors, nurses)

We all feel sick sometimes. We're going to learn that ⊠ God hears our prayers when we are sick.

Materials
paper or paper plates, markers

Option Doctor on Call

Let's explore being sick. Have you ever been sick? Allow a few children to share their stories about being sick. Ask for a volunteer to help you. Feel the child's head, take his pulse, and wrap a bandage around his arm.

- **What do people do to try to get well?** (go to a doctor, take medicine, go to a hospital, rest, sleep, drink juice)

Lay out all the toy doctor items and invite children to have fun with them, wrapping bandages on each other, pretending to take pulses and blood pressures, and so forth.

- **Who helps us when we are sick?** (moms and dads, other family members, doctors, nurses)

We all feel sick sometimes. We're going to learn that ⊠ God hears our prayers when we are sick.

Materials
bandage wraps; adhesive bandages; toy stethoscope, blood pressure cuff, etc.

Bible Memory 1 Thessalonians 5:16-18

Read aloud 1 Thessalonians 5:16-18. **How often should we rejoice?** (always) **How often should we pray?** (continually, all the time) **When should we give thanks?** (in all circumstances, always) Attach the Bible Memory shapes vertically or horizontally to a wall or bulletin board. Read the verses aloud while pointing to the words. Ask kids to join you in reading the verses while you point to the words. **Do you think we should pray when we are sick?** (yes) **We're going to learn that ⊠ God hears our prayers when we are sick.**

Materials
Bible, *Resources* Sheet 6 Bible Memory shapes, reusable adhesive or pushpins

Transition to Explore His Word
See the *Resources* CD Transition Tips printable file. As children gather, make sure you have all the materials you need.

Explore His Word (20 minutes)

Step 2 • Use all of these activities to help children **tell what Hezekiah prayed for and how God answered his prayer** and develop Bible skills.

Bible Background for the Teacher

Hezekiah was one of Judah's good kings. Hezekiah faithfully served God by restoring the temple worship that had been abandoned during the reign of his father, King Ahaz (see 2 Chronicles 28:24; 29:1-4, 35).

The time of Hezekiah's illness and impending death coincides with the time period when King Sennacherib of Assyria was preparing to invade Judah. Hezekiah's prayer for healing may have stemmed from motives that went beyond his own personal desire for physical well-being to that of the welfare of his country. He likely hoped to be able to lead Judah against the impending attacks of the Assyrians.

God answered Hezekiah's prayer and healed him by using the medicines of the time (2 Kings 20:7). God also graciously extended Hezekiah's life by 15 years. Neither God nor the prophet was angry when Hezekiah asked for a sign. He was given the choice of whether a shadow should go back or forward 10 steps. It happened just as he requested.

Worship Time

If you want to offer a time of worship, see the *Resources* CD Worship Time Ideas printable file for suggestions.

Materials

white board; dry-erase marker; Bibles; *Resources* Sheet 7 crown and Hezekiah's name 11a, story props 11b–11d; *Teaching Picture* 11; reusable adhesive

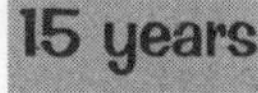
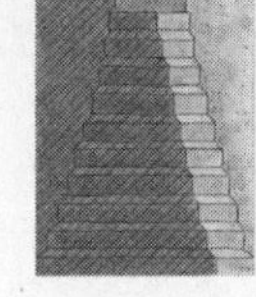

Before Class

Place 11a on the crown with reusable adhesive.

Story Option

Play the dramatized story from the *Resources* CD Track 10.

Hezekiah Prays for Healing   (2 Kings 20:1-11)

Let's think about some people from the Old Testament whom we have learned about. If you have the teaching pictures displayed, point to them while asking these questions: **What prophet had God cared for by having ravens take him food?** (Elijah) **What prophet went up against 450 prophets of Baal?** (Elijah) **What prophet did God work through to heal Naaman?** (Elisha) **What king prayed for wisdom?** (Solomon)

Write "2 Kings 20:1" on the board. **In the book of 1 and 2 Kings we learn about men who were kings. Today we are going to learn about King Hezekiah.** Help children find 2 Kings 20:11 in their Bibles and ask for a volunteer to read the first part of the verse.

You can help tell today's Bible story. Hold up the 11b Isaiah card. **When you see this card, say "Isaiah."** Hold up the 11c 15 years card. **When you see this card, say "15 years."** Hold up the crown. **When you see this crown, say "King Hezekiah."** Practice these with the children. **You also need to listen for what Hezekiah prayed for and how God answered his prayer.**

King Hezekiah prayed to God often, and he always tried to obey God. But *(hold up the crown; kids say "King Hezekiah")* became very, very sick. While he was sick, the prophet *(hold up the Isaiah card; kids say "Isaiah")* came to visit him. Isaiah told Hezekiah, "The Lord God says you are going to die. So you should put everything in order and give your last orders to everyone."

(Hold up the crown; kids say "King Hezekiah") began to pray to God. He said, "Lord, please remember that I have been faithful to you and have always obeyed You. I have done what is right and good." Then Hezekiah cried loudly. He did not want to die. *(Display* Teaching Picture *11.)*

Before *(hold up the Isaiah card; kids say "Isaiah")* left, God spoke to him. "Go back and tell Hezekiah that I have heard his prayer, and I will heal him. In three days, Hezekiah should go to the temple. And I will add *(hold up the 15 years card; kids say "15 years")* to his life. Not only that, but I will save his city and protect it."

Isaiah then had Hezekiah's servants make a paste from figs and put it on Hezekiah. And *(hold up the crown; kids say "King Hezekiah")* got well.

Hezekiah asked *(hold up the Isaiah card; kids say "Isaiah")* how he would know that God would heal him and that he should go to the temple in three days. So Isaiah asked Hezekiah, "Do you see this shadow? Do you want it to go forward or backward 10 steps?"

(Hold up the crown; kids say "King Hezekiah") thought for a moment. "It would be easy for a shadow to go forward, so let it go back 10 steps as a sign from God that He will keep His promise," Hezekiah said.

Then *(hold up the Isaiah card; kids say "Isaiah")* called to God. God made the shadow go back 10 steps! *(Show 11d.)* Hezekiah now knew that God would make him well. He knew God would keep His promise and add *(hold up the 15 years card; kids say "15 years")* to his life when he went to the temple in three days. God had heard Hezekiah's prayer. And God healed *(hold up the crown; kids say "King Hezekiah.")*

Bible Review Activity

What did Hezekiah pray for and how did God answer his prayer? (Hezekiah prayed that he would get better and not die. God gave him another 15 years to live.) **Let's see what else you remember from the Bible story as we do a fun activity.** Divide the class into two groups. Give one group the crown and tell them to stand together and say "King Hezekiah" when the statement describes King Hezekiah. Give the other group 11b and tell them to stand together and say "Isaiah" when the statement describes Isaiah. For more questions, see the Review Questions on the CD.

- **I prayed to God often.** (King Hezekiah)
- **I went to see the king when he was sick.** (Isaiah)
- **I told the king God's message that the king was going to die.** (Isaiah)
- **I did not want to die.** (King Hezekiah)
- **I told the king that God was going to heal him.** (Isaiah)
- **I asked the king if he wanted the shadow to go backward or forward 10 steps.** (Isaiah)
- **God added 15 years to my life.** (King Hezekiah)

God heard King Hezekiah's prayer when he was sick. When we get sick, we can remember that ⊠ **God hears our prayers too.**

Bible Skill Builder and Bible Memory Activity

The Bible is divided into what two main sections? (Old and New Testaments) Write "1 Thessalonians 5:16-18" on the board. **This is our Bible Memory. Is 1 Thessalonians in the Old or New Testament?** (New) **What is 1 Thessalonians?** (book of the Bible) **What is the number 5?** (chapter number) **What are the numbers 16-18?** (verse numbers) Help the children turn to 1 Thessalonians 5:16-18 in their Bibles. Ask for volunteers to read the verses.

Play "Be Joyful Always." Play again and invite kids to join in singing. Then teach kids these motions to do while singing the song: *joyful*—move an open hand from the waist to the neck; *pray*—fold hands; *thanks*—a hand touches the mouth and then moves down; *Jesus*—touch the middle finger of one hand to the middle of the palm of the other hand and then repeat with the other hand.

Our Bible Memory verses tell us that we are to pray all the time and to give thanks when we pray. And, just like King Hezekiah, ⊠ **God hears our prayers when we are sick.**

Materials 
Resources Sheet 7
crown and Isaiah
name card 11b
(optional: CD Review Questions
Unit 3 for Lesson 11 printable file)

Materials
white board, dry-
erase marker, Bibles,
Resources CD Tracks 3
and 4, CD player

Note
You may want to explain that this song is based on 1 Thessalonians 5:16-18. Although the words may differ slightly, they have the same meaning.

Make It Real (15 minutes)

Step 3 • Use one of these activities to help children **explain why it's
important to pray for people who are sick.**

Materials
white board, dry-erase
marker, construction
paper, markers

≡ *Quick Step* Praying Hands Game

**We've discovered that King Hezekiah prayed to God when he was
sick. Why is it important for us to pray for people who are sick?** As
children give reasons, list them on the board. (God hears and answers prayers.
The Bible tells us to pray for people who are sick. So they will get better.)
Distribute paper and markers. Tell kids to trace one of their hands on the
paper. Then they are to write on the hands one of the reasons to pray for sick
people.

Ask the kids to hold their praying hands and sit in a circle. Stand in the
middle of the circle. Call out one of the reasons to pray for people who are
sick and then say "Pray!" The children who have that reason written on their
papers are to change places with each other before the person in the middle
takes one of their places in the circle. Whoever is left without a place to sit can
be in the middle and call out another reason to pray for those who are sick.

**It's good to pray for people who are sick because ⊠ God hears our
prayers when we are sick.**

Materials
transparent glass or jar
filled halfway with water,
permanent marker,
effervescent antacid
tablet

Option   Rising Prayers

**We've discovered that King Hezekiah prayed to God when he was sick.
Let's explore why it's important to pray for people who are sick.** Show
kids the glass filled halfway with water. **Let's pretend that the water repre-
sents earth. The area above the water is Heaven.** Draw a happy face on the
effervescent tablet. **Let's pretend that this is you.** Drop the tablet into the
water. **Let's pretend that the bubbles represent prayers. What happens to
the prayers?** (go straight to Heaven) **The Bible tells us that our prayers do
go straight to God and that He hears and answers our prayers.**

• **Why do you think I drew a happy face on the tablet?** (We can be happy
that God hears our prayers.)

• **When you pray for someone who is sick, who hears those prayers?**
(God)

• **Why is it important to pray for people who are sick?** (God hears and
answers prayers. The Bible tells us to pray for people who are sick. So they will
get better.)

**It's good to pray for people who are sick because we know that ⊠ God
hears our prayers when we are sick.**

Materials
Weekly Bible Reader®
Issue 11

Option   Story from *Weekly Bible Reader*®

**We've discovered that King Hezekiah prayed to God when he was sick.
Let's explore why it's important to pray for people who are sick.** Read "A
Sick Neighbor."

• **Why is it important to pray for people who are sick?** (God hears and
answers prayers. The Bible tells us to pray for people who are sick. So they will
get better.)

**It's good to pray for people who are sick because we know that ⊠ God
hears our prayers when we are sick.**

Live It Out (10 minutes)

Step 4 • Use one of these activities to help children **pray for someone who is sick.**

Quick Step   Get Well Soon!

We have discovered why it's important to pray for people who are sick. So we are going to think of people we know who are sick and make them get-well cards. Then we're going to pray for them. We can pray for them because we know that ▛ God hears our prayers when we are sick. Before class, make a sample of the card. Ask kids to think of who they can make a get-well card for. Distribute the activity pages, stickers, markers, and scissors. Read the directions aloud. Have kids cut out the card and the strip at the bottom of the page. Show kids how to accordion-fold the strip on the fold lines. They can attach one of the happy face stickers on top of the folded strip and glue the folded strip inside the card so that it will pop up when the card is opened. Then kids can write messages, color the cards, decorate with the rest of the stickers, and sign their names on the cards.

Ask the children to take their cards to a closing prayer circle. Let the children share who they made their cards for. Encourage the children to pray for those people and others they know who are sick.

Option   Prayer Journal

We have discovered why it's important to pray for people who are sick. So we are going to make prayer journals that will help us remember to pray for people who are sick, and then we're going to pray for them. We can pray for them because we know that ▛ God hears our prayers when we are sick. Distribute the paper and markers. Show the children how to fold the paper in half and then in half again. Write "My Prayer Journal" on the board and ask kids to copy the title on the covers of their journals.

Have kids write in their prayer journals the names of several people who are sick. If some children don't know anyone who is sick, be prepared to give them names of people in your church who are sick. Tell the children that they should pray every day for those people. Encourage children how to write a big "thank You" by the names of people who get better.

Close with a time of prayer. Invite the children to pray for people they know who are sick.

Saying Good-bye

- Distribute Issue 11 of *Weekly Bible Reader*®.
- Make sure children have projects and activity sheets they have done.
- If you have time before parents arrive, use some of the activities on page 64.
- Remind parents that a weekly *Faith & Family* page is available online to print and use with their child at home. Go to heartshaper.com.

Materials

Activities p. 25 and corresponding stickers, markers or colored pencils, scissors, glue

Teaching Tip

Be prepared to give kids a few names of people in your church who are sick and would enjoy receiving get-well cards from the children. Be sure to mail or deliver the cards.

Materials

paper, markers, white board, dry-erase marker

Evaluate

- How did the children express confidence that God will hear and answer their prayers?
- How did you pay attention to the children who are very quiet?

Jehoshaphat Prays for Help

Bible Focus: 2 Chronicles 20:1-21, 30
Bible Memory: Rejoice always; pray continually; give thanks in all circumstances,
   for this is God's will for you in Christ Jesus (1 Thessalonians 5:16-18).
Life Focus: ⊠ God hears our prayers when we need help.

Heart to Heart

   Quick! What's the first thing you do when trouble pays you a visit? Do you panic? cry? scream? ask family and friends for help? try to fix it yourself? Jehoshaphat's first action was to call a big prayer meeting. Jehoshaphat is a great example of what to do when faced with trouble or a bad situation. He stopped everything and prayed to God for help. Not only did he pray, but he also worshiped. The next time trouble pays you a visit, be like Jehoshaphat—stop, pray, and worship. God will listen and help.

Lesson 12 at a Glance

Step 1		HeartShaper Materials	Other Materials
Focus In Use one of these activities to help children *name times they may need help.*	 *Quick Step* **Story Time** **Option In the Bag** **Bible Memory** *Use this activity to introduce the Bible Memory verses.*	• *Resources* Sheet 7 situation picture cards • none • none	• none • large paper bag, objects (see the activity) • clock, Bible
Step 2			
Explore His Word Use all of these activities to help children *tell what Jehoshaphat prayed for and how God answered his prayer* and develop Bible skills.	**Jehoshaphat Prays for Help** **Bible Review Activity** **Bible Skill Builder and Bible Memory Activity** 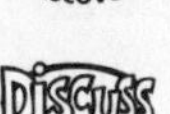	• *Resources* Sheet 7 crown, Jehoshaphat's name 12a, and story props 12b, 12c, Sheet 6 Bible Memory shapes; *Teaching Picture* 12	• white board, dry-erase marker, Bibles, reusable adhesive or pushpins
Step 3			
Make It Real Use one of these activities to help children *identify times to pray for God's help.*	 *Quick Step* **Pray for God's Help** **Option Never Stop Praying Game** 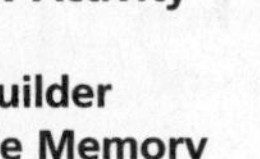 **Option Story from** *Weekly Bible Reader®* 	• *Activities* p. 27 • *Resources* Sheet 8 game board and cards for Lesson 12 • *Weekly Bible Reader®* Issue 12	• colored pencils or crayons, scissors, glue, construction paper, hole punch, yarn • small items to use as game markers, coin • none
Step 4			
Live It Out Use one of these activities to help children *plan a time to pray for God's help.*	 *Quick Step* **Pray for God's Help** **Option Pass the Picture and Pray**  **Saying Good-bye**	• *Activities* p. 27 • *Teaching Picture* 12 • *Weekly Bible Reader®* Issue 12	• none • none • none

Focus In (15 minutes)

Step 1 • Use one of these activities to help children **name times they may need help.**
Use the Bible Memory activity to introduce the memory verses.

Welcome
- Welcome each child by name.
- Do check-in procedures you follow (name and security tags, offering, attendance chart, etc.).
- Early arrivers will enjoy doing one or more of the activities described on page 64.

≡ *Quick Step*   Story Time

Let's think about times we may need help. Divide the children into four pairs or small groups. Give each group one of the situation cards. Tell the children that they are to work together to come up with stories of why the people on the cards need help. The groups can also act out their stories if they desire. After a few minutes, let the groups show the pictures and then tell the stories they have made up or act out their stories.

• **When are some other times you may need help?** (when I get hurt, when I have homework I can't do, when I don't understand the teacher's instructions, when a pet is sick, when I'm afraid of the dark, when someone has hurt my feelings, when I want to learn more about God, when I want to read the Bible)

We all need help from time to time, and there is someone who is always ready to help. We're going to discover that ☒ God hears our prayers when we need help.

Materials
Resources Sheet 7
situation picture cards

Option   In the Bag

Let's think about times we may need help. Before class, fill a bag with the suggested items. Show children the bag. Tell kids that they will pull items from the bag and name the items. Pull out the picture of a sad child. **This is a picture of someone who is sad.** Tell kids they are to use the item or picture to name a time they may need help. Example: **A time I may need help is when I'm sad because someone in my family is sick.** Have children do the same for all the items in the bag.

• **When are some other times you may need help?** (when someone has hurt my feelings, when I want to learn more about God, when I'm afraid of a big dog)

We all need help from time to time, and there is someone who is always ready to help. We're going to discover that ☒ God hears our prayers when we need help.

Materials
large paper bag; objects such as a stethoscope, picture of a storm, nightlight, thermometer, adhesive bandage, school book, picture of a pet, picture of a sad child, Bible

Bible Memory   1 Thessalonians 5:16-18

Show kids the clock and then read aloud 1 Thessalonians 5:16-18. Move the clock hands or point to the numbers as you talk about the different times. **The Bible Memory tells us to pray all the time. When it's 9 in the morning, could you pray for help? When it's noon, could you pray for help? When it's 4 in the afternoon, could you pray for help? When it's 8 in the evening, could you pray for help? We can pray whenever we need help, because ☒ God hears our prayers when we need help.**

Materials
clock, Bible

Transition to Explore His Word
See the *Resources* CD Transition Tips printable file. As children gather, make sure you have all the materials you need.

Explore His Word (20 minutes)

Step 2 • Use all of these activities to help children **tell what Jehoshaphat prayed for and how God answered his prayer** and develop Bible skills.

Bible Background for the Teacher

The response of King Jehoshaphat of Judah to the news that a vast army of enemies was headed his way was not the expected response from a king. The first thing Jehoshaphat did wasn't to gather up his troops or draw up a battle plan. Rather, he led his country in fasting and prayer. When praying for help, Jehoshaphat acknowledged God for what God had done in the past, and Jehoshaphat humbly admitted dependence upon God.

God, Judah's true commander-in-chief, responded to Jehoshaphat's prayer by reassuring Judah that the battle was the Lord's. After turning over their problem to God, King Jehoshaphat and the people did not worry—they worshiped God. This passage is a good reminder that a prayer of faith according to God's will is as good as having already received what has been prayed for (Matthew 21:21, 22).

In the end, the army of Judah did not even have to raise a hand against the enemy. God himself defeated Judah's enemy. Judah's battle had been won with prayer and praise.

Worship Time

If you want to offer a time of worship, see the *Resources* CD Worship Time Ideas printable file for suggestions.

Materials

white board; dry-erase marker; Bibles; *Resources* Sheet 7 crown, Jehoshaphat's name 12a, and story props 12b, 12c; *Teaching Picture* 12; reusable adhesive

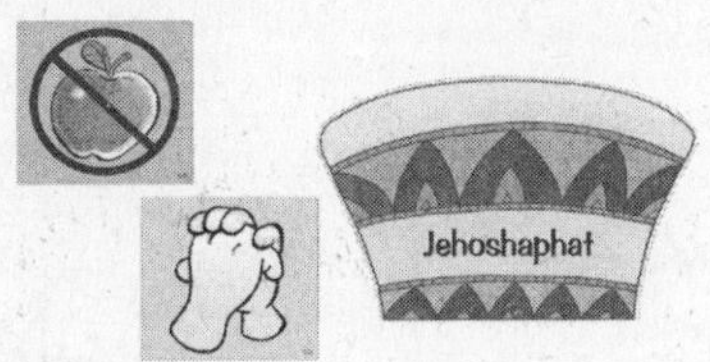

Before Class

Place 12a on the crown with reusable adhesive.

Jehoshaphat Prays for Help (2 Chronicles 20:1-21, 30)

Let's think about some people from the Old Testament whom we have learned about. If you have the quarter's teaching pictures displayed, point to them while asking these questions: **What boy defeated Goliath?** (David) **What king did David choose not to kill?** (Saul) **Who did a woman take care of by baking him a loaf of bread?** (Elijah) **Who told a woman that she and her husband would have a son?** (Elisha) **What king did God give wisdom to?** (Solomon) **What king prayed to God for healing?** (Hezekiah)

Write "2 Chronicles 20:1" on the board. **Second Chronicles also tells about men who were kings. Today we are going to learn about King Jehoshaphat** (Juh-hosh-uh-fat). Help children find 2 Chronicles 20:1 in their Bibles and ask for a volunteer to read the verse. **You can help tell the Bible story.** Hold up the crown. **When you see the crown, say "King Jehoshaphat." When you see the praying hands, say "prayed."** Practice this with the children. **Listen for what Jehoshaphat prayed for and how God answered his prayer.**

Jehoshaphat was the king in Judah. His palace was in the city of Jerusalem. *(Hold up the crown; kids say "King Jehoshaphat")* loved God and tried hard to get the people of Judah to love God too.

One day, some of the king's friends came to warn him. They said, "A huge army is coming! They are already close by."

(Hold up the crown; kids say "King Jehoshaphat") was afraid. He knew this army could be a very dangerous enemy. But Jehoshaphat did not panic. Instead, he decided to ask the Lord what they should do. Jehoshaphat told everyone in Judah that they would have a special time of prayer. No one was to eat during that time *(hold up 12b)*, so they could spend all of their time praying and thinking about God. Everyone *(hold up 12c; kids say "prayed")* to the Lord. *(Display Teaching Picture 12.)*

"O Lord," Jehoshaphat *(hold up 12c; kids say "prayed")*, "You are the king of the whole world. You are powerful and strong. You gave this land to us to live in, and here Your temple was built. Our friends and family, who lived here before us, told us that whenever times of trouble came, we should tell You all of our problems. They said You would hear our prayers and save us.

"Lord, now an enemy is coming. They want to drive us from this land. Will You help us, Lord? We can't go to war against them. We would surely lose. We don't know what to do. We are looking to You for help." God heard *(hold up the crown; kids say "King Jehoshaphat")* prayer.

Then God told Jahaziel (Juh-hay-zi-el), a godly man in the crowd, to say this: "Listen! This is what the Lord says. 'Don't be afraid or discouraged. This is not your battle; it's mine! Tomorrow, get up and go to the place where the enemy is. You won't have to fight. Just go out and the LORD will be with you.'"

(Hold up the crown; kids say "King Jehoshaphat") and all of the people bowed down and worshiped the Lord, thanking Him for hearing their prayers. Some of the people stood up and praised God with loud voices.

The next morning, Jehoshaphat's army got up early to go to the place of God's battle. *(Hold up the crown; kids say "King Jehoshaphat")* chose some men to sing and praise God while leading the army to the battleground. The singers marched in front of the army and sang, "Thank the LORD. His love continues forever." God won the battle that day. After that, God gave peace to *(Hold up the crown; kids say "King Jehoshaphat")* and his kingdom for the rest of the king's life.

Bible Review Activity

What did Jehoshaphat pray for and how did God answer Jehoshaphat's prayer? (He prayed for help as an enemy was coming to fight against them. God fought for them and won the battle.) **Let's see what else you remember from the Bible story as we act it out.** Let children act out the parts of King Jehoshaphat, the king's friends, the people, Jahaziel, and the king's army as you retell the story. Then ask a few questions:

• **What did King Jehoshaphat do as soon as he heard that an enemy was coming?** (He told everyone that there would be a special time of prayer.)

• **What did the king pray for?** (He asked for God's help.)

• **What message did God give Jahaziel to tell to the people?** (Don't be discouraged or afraid. God was going to win the battle for them.)

King Jehoshaphat prayed for help, and God answered Jehoshaphat's prayer. We're going to discover that ⊠ God hears our prayers when we need help too.

Bible Skill Builder and Bible Memory Activity

The Bible is divided into two main sections, the Old Testament and the New Testament. Find the table of contents near the front of your Bibles. Write "1 Thessalonians 5:16-18" on the board. Ask kids to point to the New Testament section and then run their fingers down the list until they find the book of 1 Thessalonians. Tell kids to find the page number 1 Thessalonians begins on and turn to it. Help them find chapter 5, verses 16-18. Ask for volunteers to read the verses.

Attach the Bible Memory shapes vertically or horizontally to a wall or bulletin board. Read the verses aloud while pointing to the words. Ask kids to join you in reading the verses while you point to the words. Then remove the Bible Memory shapes from the wall and give a shape to each child. Tell kids that they are to line up so that the words are in order. Or they can lay the shapes on a table and put them in order.

Our Bible Memory verses tell us that we are to pray all the time. Just like King Jehoshaphat, ⊠ God hears our prayers when we need help.

Make It Real (15 minutes)

Step 3 • Use one of these activities to help children **identify times to pray for God's help.**

Materials
Activities p. 27, colored pencils or crayons, scissors, glue, construction paper, hole punch, yarn

Craft

☰ *Quick Step* Pray for God's Help

We've discovered that King Jehoshaphat prayed for help and God answered Jehoshaphat's prayer. Let's think about times we can pray for God's help. Distribute the activity pages, colored pencils or crayons, scissors, and glue. Read the directions aloud. Have the children color the hands and write in the empty box other times they will pray for God's help. Then they can cut out the boxes and hands and glue onto the hands the boxes that tell times when *they* will pray for God's help. Give children half sheets of construction paper to glue their praying hands onto. Then have kids punch holes at the top of their papers and tie with yarn.

• **When are some times you will pray for God's help?** Encourage children to share the times they put on their praying hands.

Like King Jehoshaphat, there are times we need help. That's when we need to pray for God's help because we know that ⊠ God hears our prayers when we need help.

Materials
Resources Sheet 8 game board and cards for Lesson 12, small items to use as game markers, coin

Game

Teaching Tip
If you have a large class, put the children in pairs or small groups to play the game.

Option   Never Stop Praying Game

We've discovered that King Jehoshaphat prayed for help and God answered his prayer. Think about times you can pray for God's help as we play a game. Place the game board and cards on the table. Give each child a game marker. Have the first player flip a coin. If the coin is heads, the player moves one space. If it is tails, the player moves two spaces. When a player lands on a space with a star, she should draw a card and answer the question on the back of the card. Play until everyone reaches "finish" or as time allows.

• **When are some times you can pray for God's help?**

Like King Jehoshaphat, there are times we need help. That's when we need to pray for God's help because we know that ⊠ God hears our prayers when we need help.

Materials
Weekly Bible Reader® Issue 12

LISTEN

Option   Story from *Weekly Bible Reader®*

We've discovered that King Jehoshaphat prayed for help and God answered Jehoshaphat's prayer. Let's think about times we can pray for God's help. Read "Tamira."

• **When are some times you will pray for God's help?**

Like King Jehoshaphat, there are times we need help. That's when we need to pray for God's help because we know that ⊠ God hears our prayers when we need help.

Live It Out (10 minutes)

Step 4 • Use one of these activities to help children **plan a time to pray for God's help.**

≡ *Quick Step* Pray for God's Help

We've identified times we can pray for God's help. Now you need to plan a specific time you will pray for God's help. You can pray for God's help because we know that ❤ **God hears our prayers when we need help.** Have kids gather in a circle, holding the praying hands they made in the Step 3 *Quick Step* activity. If you did not have kids do this activity in Step 3, have them do it now.

Look at the times to pray for God's help that you put on your praying hands. Choose one of those times. Now share with the group one of the times you plan on praying for God's help by saying something like the following: I plan to pray for God's help before taking a test. After each child has shared, ask a question such as, **The next test you have, what will you first plan to do?** or **The next time you get sick, what will you first plan to do?**

Close with a time of prayer. Encourage children to pray and thank God for the help He gives.

Materials
Activities p. 27

Option   Pass the Picture and Pray

We've identified times we can pray for God's help. Now you need to plan a specific time you will pray for God's help. You can pray for God's help because we know that ❤ **God hears our prayers when we need help.** Ask the children to sit in a circle. **As a reminder that King Jehoshaphat prayed for God's help, we're going to pass this picture of Jehoshaphat around the circle. When you get the picture, name a time you will ask for God's help.** Then lead the class in prayer. **Dear God, please help ___** (name of child) **when she needs help ___** (time the child named). Then the child can pass the picture to the next person. Make sure each child gets to name a time she will ask for God's help and that you pray for each child.

Materials
Teaching Picture 12

Added Fun!
Play "Be Joyful Always"
from the *Resources* CD Tracks 3 and 4 and invite kids to join in singing to thank God for hearing our prayers.

Saying Good-bye
• Distribute Issue 12 of *Weekly Bible Reader*®.
• Make sure children have projects and activity sheets they have done.
• If you have time before parents arrive, use some of the activities on page 64.
• Remind parents that a weekly *Faith & Family* page is available online to print and use with their child at home. Go to heartshaper.com.

Evaluate
• How willing are the children to pray aloud?
• How well are you getting to know the children in your class?

Manasseh Prays for Forgiveness

13

Bible Focus: 2 Chronicles 33:1-20
Bible Memory: Rejoice always; pray continually; give thanks in all circumstances,
   for this is God's will for you in Christ Jesus (1 Thessalonians 5:16-18).
Life Focus: ⊠ God hears our prayers when we need forgiveness.

Heart to Heart
   God's dealing with Manasseh is one of the best examples we have of God's merciful forgiveness. God not only forgave him of all his evil doings, but God blessed him beyond measure. Let the story of Manasseh and God's forgiveness give you hope! No matter how bad or evil you have been, God will forgive a sincere and truly repentant heart. Let go of any pride you may have and ask God for His forgiveness. He will forgive. That's a promise!

Lesson 13 at a Glance

Step 1		HeartShaper Materials	Other Materials
Focus In Use one of these activities to help children *explore forgiveness*.	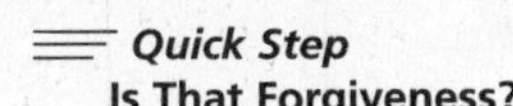 *Quick Step* **Is That Forgiveness?**	• none	• none
	Option Path of Forgiveness 	• reproducible p. 96	• markers
	Bible Memory *Use this activity to introduce the Bible Memory verses.* 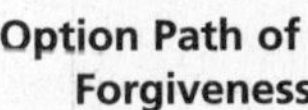	• *Resources* Sheet 6 Bible Memory shapes	• Bible, reusable adhesive or pushpins

Step 2			
Explore His Word Use all of these activities to help children *tell what Manasseh prayed for and how God answered his prayer* and develop Bible skills.	**Manasseh Prays for Forgiveness**  **Bible Review Activity**  **Bible Skill Builder and Bible Memory Activity** 	• *Resources* Sheet 7 crown, Manasseh's name 13a, and story props 13b–13d, CD Review Questions Unit 3 printable file and Tracks 3 and 4; *Teaching Picture* 13; *Activities* p. 30	• white board, dry-erase marker, Bibles, reusable adhesive, pencils, CD player

Step 3			
Make It Real Use one of these activities to help children *list times to pray for God's forgiveness*.	 *Quick Step* **Please Forgive**	• *Activities* p. 29	• pencils, white board, dry-erase marker
	Option Never Stop Praying Game 	• *Resources* Sheet 8 game board and cards for Lesson 13	• small items to use as game markers, coin, white board, dry-erase marker
	Option Story from *Weekly Bible Reader* 	• *Weekly Bible Reader*® Issue 13	• white board, dry-erase marker

Step 4			
Live It Out Use one of these activities to help children *pray for forgiveness*.	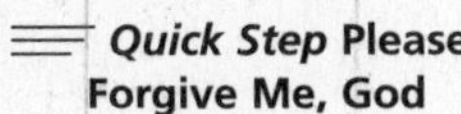 *Quick Step* **Please Forgive Me, God**	• none	• none
	Option Prayers of Forgiveness 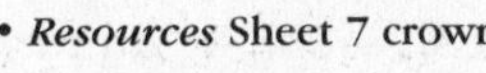	• *Resources* Sheet 7 crown	• none
	Saying Good-bye	• *Weekly Bible Reader*® Issue 13	• none

Life Focus
⊠ God hears our prayers when we need forgiveness.

Step 1 • Use one of these activities to help children **explore forgiveness.**
Use the Bible Memory activity to introduce the memory verses.

Welcome
- Welcome each child by name.
- Do check-in procedures you follow (name and security tags, offering, attendance chart, etc.).
- Early arrivers will enjoy doing one or more of the activities described on page 64.

Quick Step   Is That Forgiveness?

Let's explore forgiveness. As I read a sentence, decide if the person is showing forgiveness or not. If the person is showing forgiveness, stand up and look happy. If the person is not showing forgiveness, stay seated and look sad. Have the kids sit down after each sentence if they are standing. Make up more situations as time allows.

Nicole accidentally broke her brother's toy. He is still very angry with her. (stay seated)

Joshua's mom broke a promise to him. She said she was sorry. Joshua said that it was OK and gave his mom a hug. (stand up)

Ethan's sister said something mean to him. She said she was sorry. Ethan is angry and is planning to say something mean to her. (stay seated)

Keisha accidentally stepped on Allie's foot. Keisha said she was sorry. Allie said it was OK. (stand up)

- **Have you ever forgiven someone? How did you show you forgave?**
- **What does it mean to forgive someone?** (You don't stay angry with someone who has hurt you. You quit feeling bad about that person.)

We all need forgiveness from time to time. We're going to learn that ⊠ God hears our prayers when we need forgiveness.

Materials
none

Added Fun!
Let the kids make up situations to say to the rest of the class.

Option   Path of Forgiveness

Let's explore forgiveness as we do a fun activity. Before class, make copies of the reproducible page. Distribute the reproducible pages and markers. Tell kids that you will read the sentences in order and they will award themselves points. 1. **If you have ever forgiven someone for being mean to you, give yourself 1 point.** Kids should write a "1" on the blank line. 2. **If you have ever asked your mom and dad to forgive you, give yourself 1 point.** Do the same with all the sentences. Encourage kids to be truthful. When finished, kids may enjoy sharing how many points they got.

- **What does it mean to forgive someone?** (You don't stay angry with someone who has hurt you. You quit feeling bad about that person.)

We all have a lot to learn about forgiveness because we all need forgiveness from time to time. We're going to learn that ⊠ God hears our prayers when we need forgiveness.

Materials
reproducible p. 96, markers

Teaching Tip
You may want to let children, especially advanced readers, read the sentences.

Bible Memory   1 Thessalonians 5:16-18

Read aloud 1 Thessalonians 5:16-18. Attach the Bible Memory shapes vertically or horizontally to a wall or bulletin board. Ask kids to join you in reading the verses while you point to the words. Then remove the Bible Memory shapes from the wall and give a shape to each child. Tell kids that they are to line up so that the words are in order. Or they can lay the shapes on a table and put them in order. **Do you think we should pray when we need forgiveness?** (yes) **We're going to learn that ⊠ God hears our prayers when we need forgiveness.**

Materials
Bible, *Resources* Sheet 6 Bible Memory shapes, reusable adhesive or pushpins

Transition to Explore His Word
See the *Resources* CD Transition Tips printable file. As children gather, make sure you have all the materials you need.

Explore His Word (20 minutes)

Step 2 • Use all of these activities to help children **tell what Manasseh prayed for and how God answered his prayer** and develop Bible skills.

Bible Background for the Teacher

Manasseh, Judah's longest reigning king, assumed the throne at age 12 and reigned for 55 years. Unfortunately, for most of those years, Manasseh was possibly Judah's most wicked king (see 2 Chronicles 33:9). His catalog of sins included reestablishing the worship places devoted to Baal that Manasseh's father, good King Hezekiah, had destroyed; worshiping the sun, moon, and stars; and actively participating in practices of the occult. He was a mass murderer, taking the lives of those who morally opposed him (see 2 Kings 21:16) and murdering his own sons in child sacrifice to the false god Molech.

Desiring to discipline rather than destroy, God permitted Manasseh to be taken captive by the Assyrians to the city of Babylon where Manasseh finally repented and humbly cried out to God for forgiveness. And true to His nature, God forgave Manasseh, allowing him to return to Jerusalem to continue his reign as king. The fruits of Manasseh's repentance are seen in the fact that he removed the objects of Judah's idolatrous worship and restored the worship of the one true God.

Worship Time

If you want to offer a time of worship, see the *Resources* CD Worship Time Ideas printable file for suggestions.

Materials

white board; dry-erase marker; Bibles; *Resources* Sheet 7 crown, Manasseh's name 13a, and story props 13b–13d; *Teaching Picture* 13; reusable adhesive

Before Class

Place 13a on the crown with reusable adhesive.

Manasseh Prays for Forgiveness   (2 Chronicles 33:1-20)

Let's think about some kings from the Old Testament whom we have learned about. These kings all prayed to God. Let all the kids shout out the answers together. **What king prayed for wisdom?** (Solomon) **What king prayed for healing?** (Hezekiah) **What king prayed for help?** (Jehoshaphat)

Write "2 Chronicles 33:1" on the board. **Second Chronicles tells us about one more king, King Manasseh** (Muh-nass-uh). Help children find 2 Chronicles 33:1 in their Bibles and ask for a volunteer to read the verse. **You can help tell today's Bible story.** Hold up the crown. **When you see this crown, say "King Manasseh."** Hold up the stars card. **When you see this card, say "stars."** Hold up the chains card. **When you see this card, say "chains."** Practice these with the children. **You also need to listen for what Manasseh prayed for and how God answered Manasseh's prayer.**

(Hold up 13b.) Manasseh was only 12 years old when his father, King Hezekiah, died. Manasseh became the king of Judah, but he forgot how kind God had been to his father. As *(hold up the crown; kids say "King Manasseh")* grew older, he began to do more and more bad things that hurt God. He did three very evil things. Manasseh began to build idols for the people to worship instead of God. He forgot who made the *(hold up the stars card; kids say "stars")* and he worshiped the *(hold up the stars card; kids say "stars")* instead of God. And Manasseh even had some of his own sons killed.

God tried to speak to *(hold up the crown; kids say "King Manasseh")* and the people of Judah, but not one person would listen. God had to get their attention. He brought some enemies of Judah to Jerusalem and they took King Manasseh prisoner. The soldiers put heavy *(hold up the chains card; kids say "chains")* on the king's legs and wrists. Then they led the king away to a country far from his home.

(Hold up the crown; kids say "King Manasseh") was scared and lonely. He knew there was no one in all of Judah who could save him—not his best fighting men, not his whole army, not a surprise attack, not a big war. Not one person could save him now.

Then *(hold up the crown; kids say "King Manasseh")* remembered that one person could save Him—God. Manasseh probably thought about all of the times that God had saved His people from their enemies. God could save him!

But he had not loved and served God as he should have. *(Hold up the crown; kids say "King Manasseh")* was ashamed and embarrassed. He had to tell God he was sorry. He began to pray and tell God how very sorry he was for all of the bad things he had done in Judah—things that had hurt God. This was just the thing that God was waiting to hear.

To show *(Hold up the crown; kids say "King Manasseh")* that God had heard his prayer, God allowed Manasseh to go back to Jerusalem to be king once more. And this time, Manasseh had changed! Manasseh wanted to please God instead of hurt Him. *(Hold up the crown; kids say "King Manasseh")* tore down the idols and rebuilt a stronger wall around God's city, Jerusalem. Manasseh and his people began to worship and serve the one true God once again.

(Hold up the crown; kids say "King Manasseh") was king of Judah for 55 years. He was king in Judah longer than any other king. Manasseh's life had a happy ending because *(hold up the crown; kids say "King Manasseh")* told God he was sorry, and God heard and answered Manasseh's prayer.

Bible Review Activity

What did Manasseh pray for and how did God answer his prayer? (He prayed for forgiveness. God forgave Manasseh and let him return to Jerusalem to be the king again.) **Let's see what else you remember from the Bible story.** Distribute the activity pages and pencils. Read the directions aloud and do the page together. Then have the children gather in a circle to play this game. Tell the kids that they will pass the crown around the circle until you say "King Manasseh." Whoever is holding the crown should put it on while you ask him a question about the Bible story.

- **How old was Manasseh when he became king?** (12 years old)
- **What did Manasseh worship instead of God?** (the stars)
- **After Manasseh was taken prisoner, who did he realize could save him?** (God)
- **Why did Manasseh pray to God?** (to ask for forgiveness for all the wrong things he had done)
- **What did Manasseh do when God let him become king again?** (tore down the idols and rebuilt a stronger wall around Jerusalem)

Manasseh prayed for forgiveness and God forgave him. ⌧ God hears our prayers when we need forgiveness too.

Bible Skill Builder and Bible Memory Activity

The Bible is divided into what two main sections? (Old and New Testament) Write "1 Thessalonians 5:16-18" on the board. Ask for volunteers to put a circle around the Bible book, a square around the chapter number, and a triangle around the verse numbers. Help children find 1 Thessalonians 5:16-18 in their Bibles. Ask for volunteers to read the verses.

Play "Be Joyful Always" and invite kids to join in singing. Remind kids of motions to do while singing: *joyful*—move an open hand from the waist to the neck; *pray*—fold hands; *thanks*—a hand touches the mouth and then moves down; *Jesus*—touch the middle finger of one hand to the middle of the palm of the other hand and then repeat with the other hand.

Lead the kids in saying the Bible Memory verses together. Give time for those children who would like to say the verses by themselves.

Our Bible Memory verses tell us that we are to pray all the time and to give thanks when we pray. Just like King Manasseh, ⌧ God hears our prayers when we need forgiveness.

Materials
Activities p. 30; pencils; *Resources* Sheet 7 crown, CD Review Questions Unit 3 for Lesson 13 printable file

Teaching Tip
For more questions, see the Unit 3 Review Questions for Lesson 13 on the CD.

Materials
white board, dry-erase marker, Bibles, *Resources* CD Tracks 3 and 4, CD player

Make It Real (15 minutes)

Step 3 • Use one of these activities to help children **list times to pray for forgiveness.**

Materials
Activities p. 29, pencils, white board, dry-erase marker

Activity Page

≡ *Quick Step* Please Forgive

We've learned that King Manasseh prayed for forgiveness and God answered Manasseh's prayer. Let's think about times we can pray for forgiveness. Distribute the activity pages and pencils. Read the directions aloud and do the page together. Guide children to write their own prayers at the bottom of the page.

• **How do we ask God for forgiveness?** (pray and tell him wrong things we have done and ask for His forgiveness)

• **When are some other times you can pray and ask for forgiveness?** (when we lie, disobey parents or teachers, treat others badly, steal, are angry with others, break a promise) List these on the board.

There are many times we will need to pray for forgiveness. Remember that ⊠ God hears our prayers when we need forgiveness.

Materials
Resources Sheet 8 game board and cards for Lesson 13, small items to use as game markers, coin, white board, dry-erase marker

Game

Teaching Tip
If you have a large class, put the children in pairs or small groups to play the game.

Option Never Stop Praying Game

We've discovered that King Manasseh prayed for forgiveness and God answered Manasseh's prayer. Think about times you can pray for God's forgiveness as we play a game. Place the game board and cards on the table. Give each child a game marker. Have the first player flip a coin. If the coin is heads, the player moves one space. If it is tails, the player moves two spaces. When a player lands on a space with a star, he should draw a card and answer the question on the back of the card. Play until everyone reaches "finish" or as time allows.

• **When are some times you can pray for God's forgiveness?** List these on the board.

Like King Manasseh, there are times we need forgiveness. That's when you need to pray for God's forgiveness because we know that ⊠ God hears our prayers when we need forgiveness.

Materials
Weekly Bible Reader® Issue 13, white board, dry-erase marker

Option Story from *Weekly Bible Reader®*

We've learned that King Manasseh prayed for forgiveness and God answered Manasseh's prayer. Let's think about times we can pray for forgiveness. Read "A Sneaky Snack."

• **When are some times you can pray and ask for forgiveness?** (when we lie, disobey parents or teachers, treat others badly, steal, are angry with others, break a promise) List these on the board.

There are many times we will need to pray for forgiveness. Remember that ⊠ God hears our prayers when we need forgiveness.

Step 4 • Use one of these activities to help children **pray for forgiveness.**

Quick Step   Please Forgive Me, God

We have listed some times we need to pray for God's forgiveness. We're going to pray right now because we know that ⊠ God hears our prayers when we need forgiveness. Have children gather for a prayer circle. Tell kids that you will pray a line, and then they should respond by praying "Please forgive me, God."

Teacher:	**Dear God, I'm sorry for the times I have lied.**
Children:	Please forgive me, God.
Teacher:	**I'm sorry for the times I have not played by the rules.**
Children:	Please forgive me, God.
Teacher:	**I'm sorry for the times I have cheated.**
Children:	Please forgive me, God.
Teacher:	**I'm sorry for the times I have disobeyed my parents.**
Children:	Please forgive me, God.
Teacher:	**I'm sorry for the times when I have broken my promises.**
Children:	Please forgive me, God.
Teacher:	**I'm sorry for the times I have been angry with others.**
Children:	Please forgive me, God.
Teacher:	**I'm sorry for the times I have not been kind to others.**
Children:	Please forgive me, God.
Teacher:	**Thank You, God, for hearing our prayers and forgiving us. In Jesus' name, amen.**

Materials
none

Added Fun!
Play "Show My Love" from the *Resources* CD Tracks 5 and 6 and invite kids to join in singing to thank God for hearing our prayers.

Teaching Tip
You can also pray about other times that kids mentioned in Step 3.

Option   Prayers of Forgiveness

We have listed some times we need to pray for God's forgiveness. We're going to pray right now because we know that ⊠ God hears our prayers when we need forgiveness. Have the children sit in a circle. Tell the children they will pass around the crown. When each child gets the crown, he should hold it or put it on and silently pray for God's forgiveness. When he is done praying, he should gently tap the next child and lay the crown in his lap. Remind the children that they should bow their heads and close their eyes during the prayer time. After all the children have prayed silently, close by praying, **Thank You, God, for hearing our prayers and forgiving us. In Jesus' name, amen.**

Materials
Resources Sheet 7 crown

Saying Good-bye

• Distribute Issue 13 of *Weekly Bible Reader®* and the *Activities* page 31 Unit 3 Bible Memory poster and stickers if you have not already done so. Also distribute the *Activities* Mystery Ink pages if you have not done so already.

• Make sure children have projects and activity sheets they have done.

• If you have time before parents arrive, use some of the activities on page 64.

• Remind parents that a weekly *Faith & Family* page is available online to print and use with their child at home. Go to heartshaper.com.

Evaluate
• How did the children demonstrate that they understood the importance of praying for God's forgiveness?

• Take some extra time to evaluate. What things will you continue doing? What things will you change to better meet the needs of the children in your class?

1. In each section, draw or write about a
   job you have.
2. Cut out the wheel.
3. Punch a hole near the top.
4. String with yarn and tie. Hang the
   wheel at home as a reminder to thank
   God for helping you with your jobs.

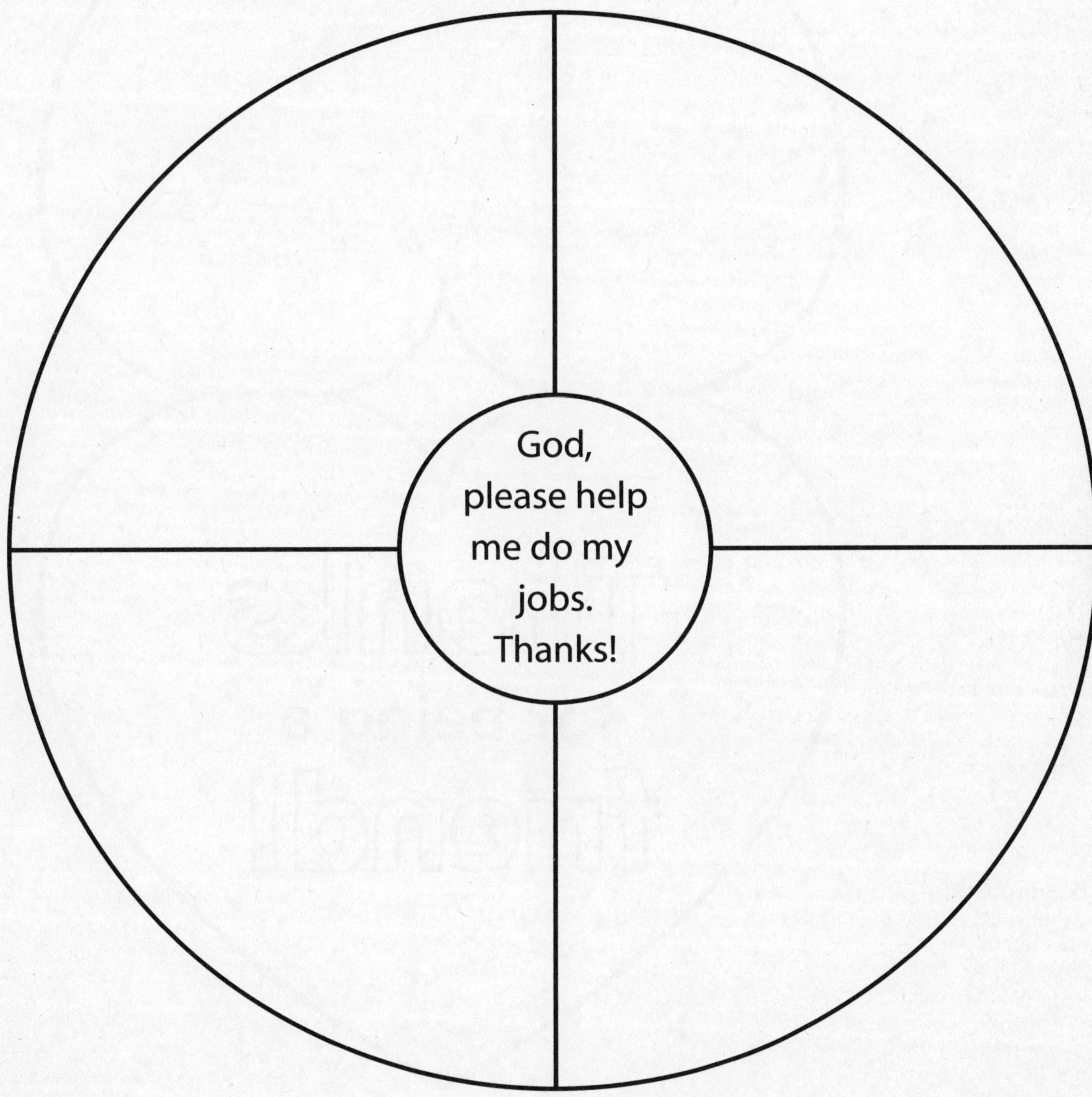

Use with Lesson 1.

Early Elementary Teacher, HeartShaper® Curriculum

1. Cut out the hearts.
2. Fold on the lines.
3. Write a friendly message inside.
4. Color and decorate the hearts. Then give your card to a friend.

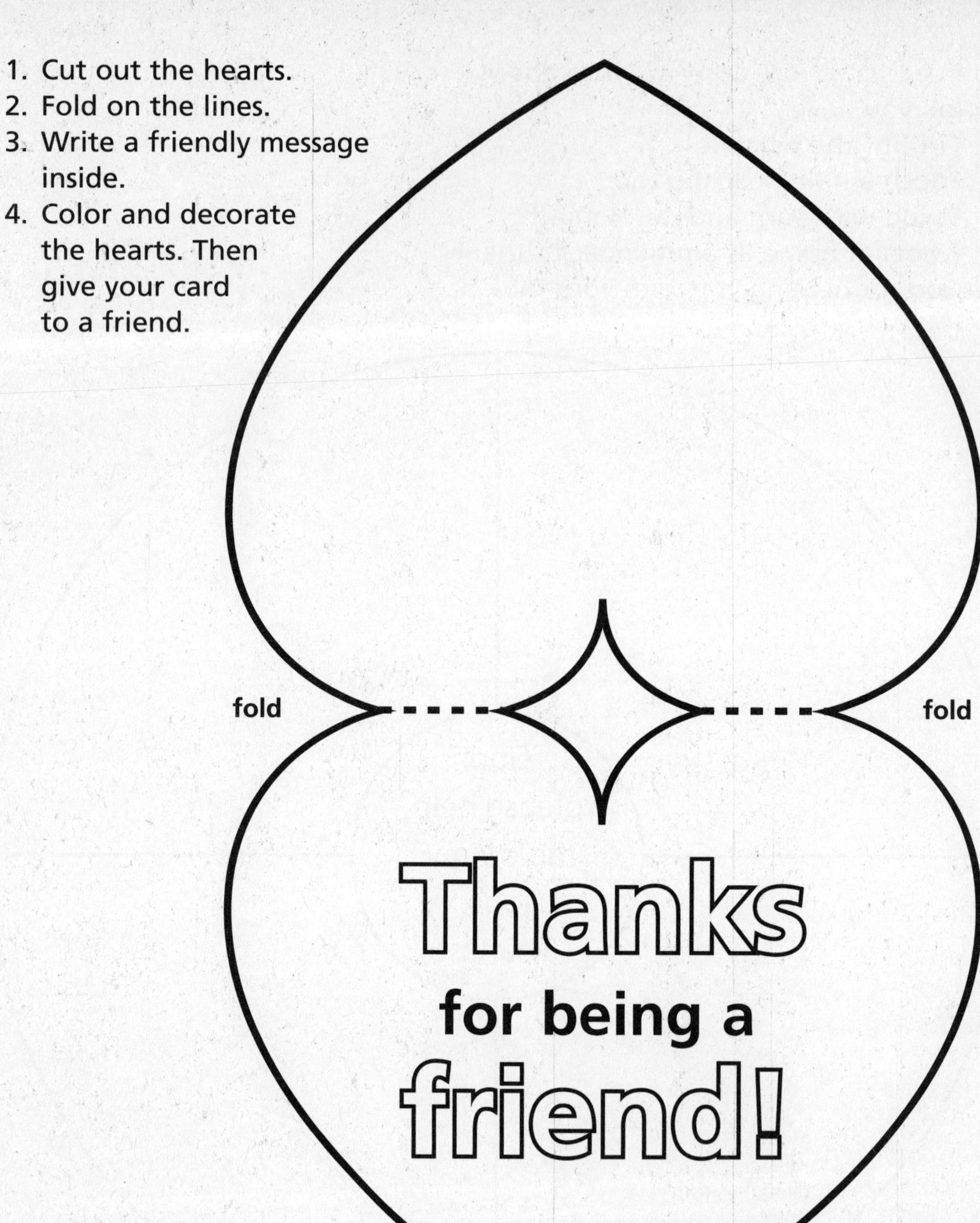

1. Cut out the pennant.
2. Glue on pictures from the *Activities* page.
3. Color and decorate your pennant.

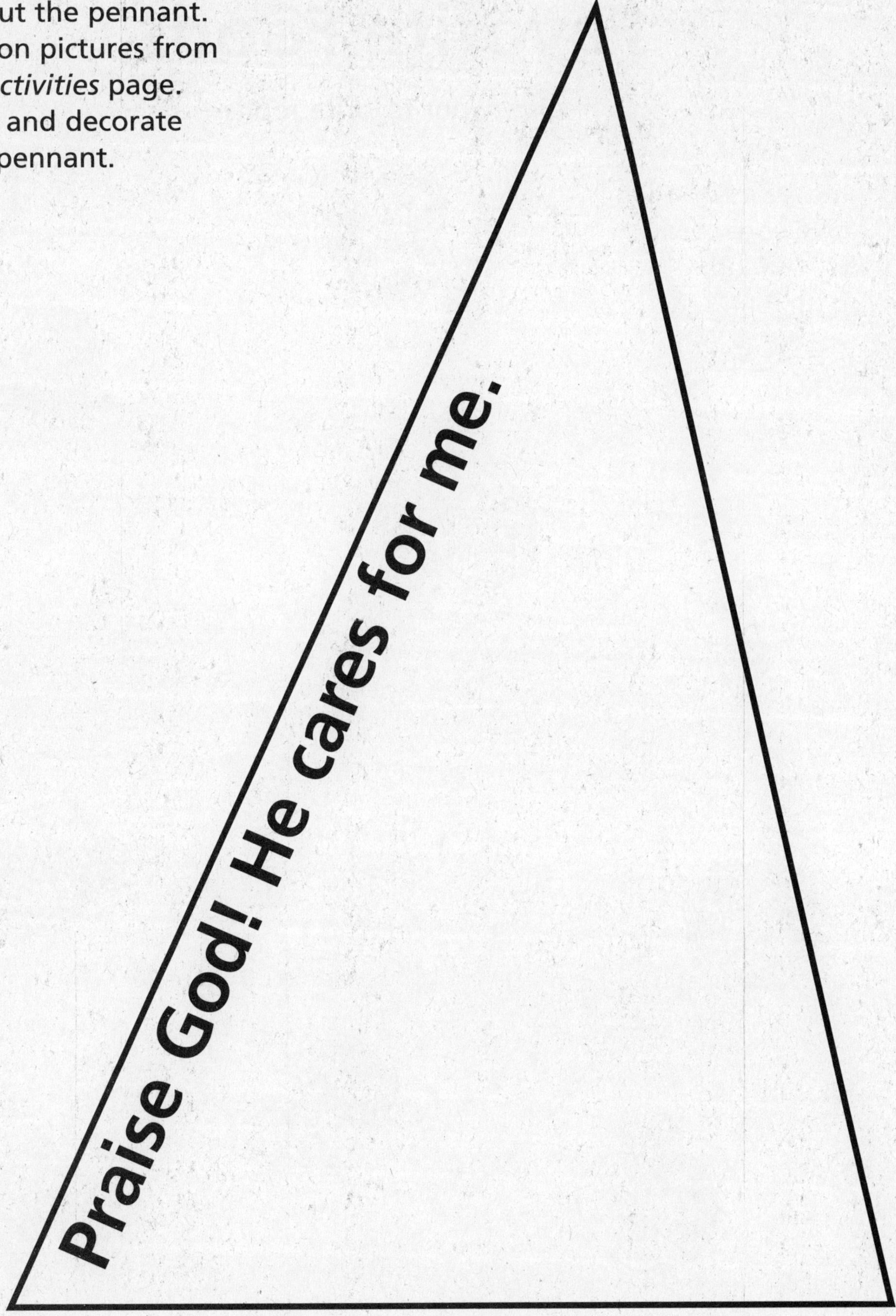

Use with Lesson 5.

Early Elementary Teacher, HeartShaper® Curriculum
Permission is granted to reproduce this page for ministry purposes only—not for resale.

Favorite Foods

Circle your favorite foods.

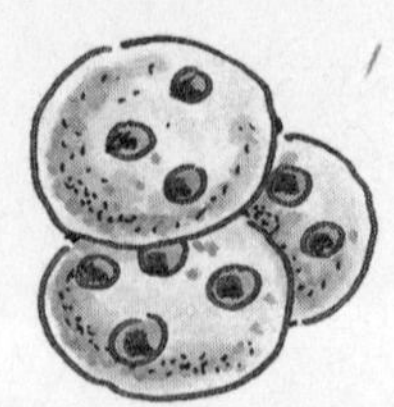

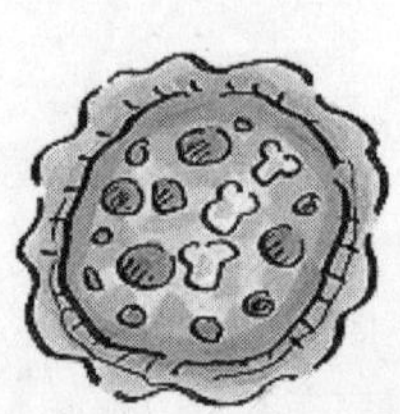

Use with Lesson 6.

Early Elementary Teacher, HeartShaper® Curriculum
Permission is granted to reproduce this page for ministry purposes only—not for resale.

1. Cut out the cube on the solid lines.
2. Fold the cube on the dotted lines.
3. Tape the edges together.

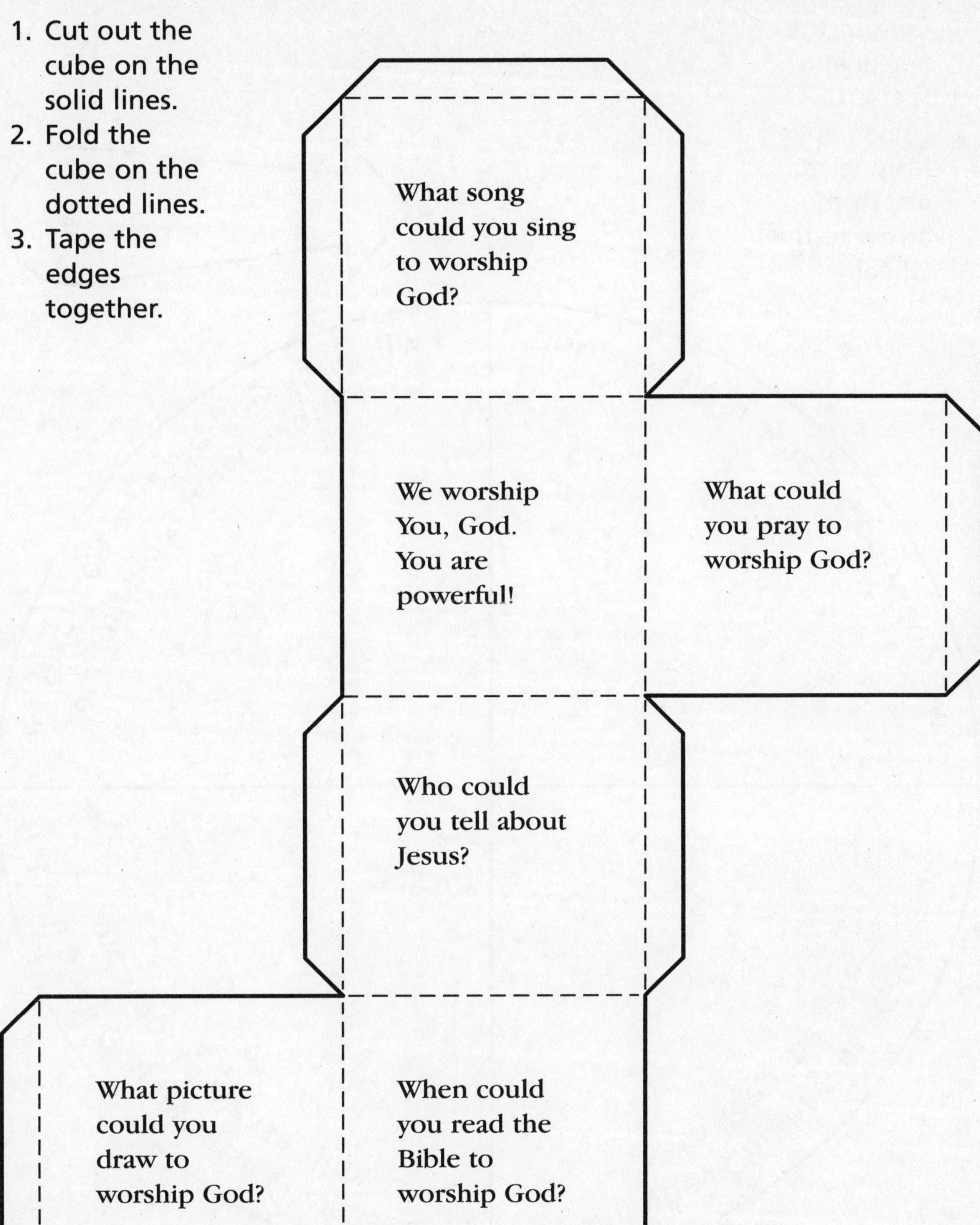

Use with Lesson 7.

1. Cut out the wheel and the arrow.
2. Use a paper fastener to attach the arrow to the wheel.

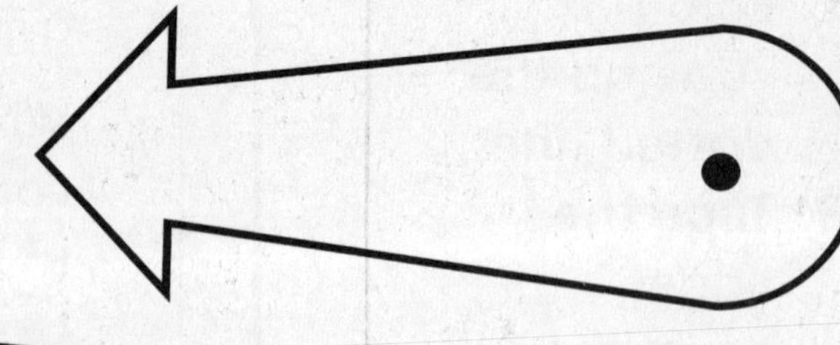

I will obey God because it pleases God.

I will obey God because God loves me and knows what is best for me.

I will obey God because God wants to keep me safe.

I will obey God because I love God and want to please Him.

1. Color the pennants.
2. Cut them out.
3. Attach to straws or craft sticks.

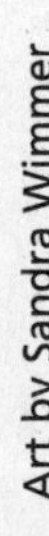

Use with Lesson 10.

Early Elementary Teacher, HeartShaper® Curriculum

Path of Forgiveness

Start   **Finish**

1. If you have ever forgiven someone for being mean to you, give yourself 1 point.

____

7. If you have ever forgiven a family member for lying to you, give yourself 1 point.

____

2. If you have ever asked your mom and dad to forgive you, give yourself 1 point.

____

6. If you have ever asked a brother, sister, or family member to forgive you for being angry with them, give yourself 1 point.

____

3. If you have ever forgiven a friend for breaking a promise to you, give yourself 1 point.

____

4. If you have ever told someone you were sorry for saying something mean, give yourself 1 point.

____

5. If you have ever forgiven someone or someone has forgiven you, give yourself 1 point.

____